Semi-Monde

'Only in *Semi-Monde* does Coward find a successful metaphor for the sexual complications that lie behind his posturing. *Semi-Monde* is easily the most visually daring of his comedies, and the most intellectually startling ... made up of sexually mischievous *tableaux vivants* it gets much nearer the homosexual knuckle than Coward's public image allowed.'
John Lahr, *London Review of Books*

Written in 1926 and originally entitled *Ritz Bar*, *Semi-Monde* was considered too daring for its time, '... its production in London or New York seemed unlikely as some of the characters, owing to lightly suggested abormalities, would certainly be deleted by the censor.' (Noël Coward, *Present Indicative*) It received its premiere at the Citizens Theatre, Glasgow, in September 1977.

NOËL COWARD

SEMI-MONDE

Methuen

Methuen

1 3 5 7 9 10 8 6 4 2

First published in *Noël Coward Collected Plays: Six*
in 1999 by Methuen Publishing Limited

This single edition published by Methuen Publishing Limited
215 Vauxhall Bridge Road, London SW1V 1EJ

Methuen Publishing Limited Reg. No. 3543167

A CIP catalogue record for this book
is available from the British Library

ISBN 0 413 76300 5

Typeset by Deltatype Limited, Birkenhead, Merseyside

Printed and bound in Great Britain by
Cox and Wyman Ltd, Reading, Berkshire

Caution

SEMI-MONDE

CHARACTERS

Tanis Marshall
Day Porter
Young Girl
Young Man
Dorothy Price
Suzanne Fellini
Mike Craven
Mr. Fletcher
Mrs. Fletcher
Beryl Fletcher
Beverley Ford
Cyril Hardacre
Albert Hennick
Owen Marshall
Inez Zulieta
Cynthia Gable
Marion Fawcett
Jerome Kennedy
Norma Kennedy
Julius Levenovitch
Elise Trent
Harry Leftwich
George Hudd
Maître d'Hôtel
Two Barmen
Luke Bellows
Joshua Drake
Benny Tyrell
Freddy Palmer
Violet Emery

MR. JEVON
MRS. JEVON
MR. HANCOX
MRS. HANCOX
PHYLLIS HANCOX
EDGAR DARRELL
WAITERS, LIFT-BOYS, HOTEL GUESTS, *etc.*

The action of the play passes in a hotel in Paris.

ACT I—1924

Scene I.   The Lounge (Place du Cœur). January. Late afternoon.

Scene II. Communicating passage between Place du Cœur and Rue Gilon sides. A few days later—before lunch.

Scene III. The Bar—lunch time—March.

ACT II—1925

Scene I.   The Lounge (Rue Gilon side). January. After lunch.

Scene II. The Bar again. February. Before lunch.

Scene III. Corner of the terrace outside the Grill Room. June—lunch time.

ACT III—1926

Scene I.   The Men's Bar—before dinner—January.

Scene II. The Lounge (Rue Gilon side). The same night. 3 a.m.

Scene III. The Lounge (Place du Cœur). June. Late afternoon.

NOTE

Whoever produces this play must use his own discretion as to the breaking up of scenes by various necessary interruptions, such as the entrances and exits of non-speaking parts, at places in which he considers such interruptions least harmful to the action. I have purposely minimised my stage directions realising that grouping and movement in a production of this sort can only satisfactorily be decided in actual rehearsal.

ACT I

Scene I

Time: *January 1924. Late afternoon.*
Scene: *The Reading and Waiting Room of a hotel in Paris. The Bureau, lifts and doors opening onto Place du Cœur are in the background. The foreground is occupied by a small writing desk and a few chairs, also a table strewn with periodicals.*

When the curtain rises, Tanis Marshall *is seated at writing desk writing postcards. A* Young Girl *is seated near by looking through an illustrated weekly. She occasionally looks up as though expecting someone. The swing doors admit two people, a man and woman, who pass across the back on their way to tea. Music can be heard from the tea lounge. At last the* Young Man *she is expecting comes in. She half rises and then goes on reading the paper as though she hadn't seen him; he approaches her.*

Young Man: I'm terribly sorry.
Young Girl: I've been here for ages.
Young Man: Please forgive me. I couldn't get away.
Young Girl: It doesn't matter.
Young Man: Where shall we go?
Young Girl: Anywhere.
Young Man: The same as last time?
Young Girl: If you like.

YOUNG MAN: You're not really angry, are you?

YOUNG GIRL: I do hate waiting about.

YOUNG MAN: It can't be helped, you know, really—
every now and then I have to be so damned careful.

YOUNG GIRL: So have I.

YOUNG MAN: Sweetheart!

YOUNG GIRL (*taking his arm, half smiling*): Shhh!
They go out.

TANIS *beckons to the* DAY PORTER, *who is
standing just by the swing doors. He comes over to
her.*

TANIS: Mr. Marshall hasn't come in yet, has he?

DAY PORTER: No, madam.

TANIS: When he does, tell him I'm in here, in case he
doesn't see me.

DAY PORTER: Yes, madam.
He goes back and takes up his stand by the doors.
DOROTHY PRICE *and* SUZANNE FELLINI *come out
from the direction of the lifts and stand talking.*
DOROTHY PRICE *is chic, beautifully dressed, on the
flashy side.* SUZANNE *is also well dressed but less
ostentatious.*

DOROTHY: He makes me tired—he really does.

SUZANNE: Why argue with him?

DOROTHY: He's so damned pig-headed.

SUZANNE: Wait until we get to Zoë's and he's had a
cocktail or two, then all will be well.

DOROTHY: He's more trouble than he's worth.

SUZANNE (*laughing*): Don't be silly, dear!

DOROTHY (*almost laughing too*): I don't know what I
should do without you, Suzanne. Honestly I don't; you
must come to Cannes with us.

SUZANNE: He'd hate the sight of me in a week.

6

DOROTHY: That doesn't matter—I can manage him.

SUZANNE: There are other reasons too why I can't come.

DOROTHY: I can arrange all that.

SUZANNE: You mean you can make him arrange it.

DOROTHY: Well, it doesn't matter, does it, as long as you're there? You must come. I shall go mad, if you don't.

SUZANNE: Here he is—for God's sake be a little nicer to him.

MIKE CRAVEN *comes from the lift, small but rather pugnacious looking.*

DOROTHY: Did you find it?

MIKE: Yes, here it is. (*He gives her a small cigarette box.*) I had to search the room out for it.

DOROTHY (*sweetly*): I'm so sorry, Mike dear.

The FLETCHERS *arrive. The* PORTER *brings in their hand luggage.* MRS. FLETCHER *is stout and rich middle-class American.* MR. FLETCHER *is spare and appears depressed.* BERYL *is young, rather over-smart and extremely lovely. She stares at* DOROTHY *with great interest.*

MIKE: We'd better be moving along, hadn't we—we can't stand about here all day.

DOROTHY: I should hate to, darling. (*She winks at* SUZANNE.)

As they go out of the swing doors——

MR. FLETCHER (*in uneasy French*): Il ya un autre valise encore.

DAY PORTER (*in perfect English*): Very well, sir. I will get it. (*He motions him towards the Bureau.*)

BERYL: Did you see her bangles, Mother?

MRS. FLETCHER: Whose bangles?

BERYL: The woman that just went out.

MRS. FLETCHER: I do hope they've made the reservations all right.

BERYL: They were heavenly—and that little cigarette case was darling.

MRS. FLETCHER: I know what European hotels are like . . .

They disappear in the direction of the Bureau, where MR. FLETCHER *is talking to the* ASSISTANT MANAGER.

BEVERLEY FORD and CYRIL HARDACRE come through the swing doors, carrying small bags and followed by the DAY PORTER, carrying their larger ones. BEVERLEY is about forty, extremely well dressed.

CYRIL is in his twenties—good-looking and slim.

BEVERLEY (*to the DAY PORTER*): Pay the taxi, will you? I haven't any change.

DAY PORTER (*putting down the bags*): Yes, sir.

CYRIL: I have.

BEVERLEY: No—he'll do it.

The DAY PORTER goes out.

Well, my dear—here we are at last. Paris is a virgin for you, unsullied by memories. Are you happy?

CYRIL (*with faint impatience*): Of course I am.

BEVERLEY (*with a giggle*): You blush so beautifully when I make affected remarks.

CYRIL: Oh shut up, Beverley.

BEVERLEY: That's why I make them.

ALBERT HENNICK enters from the direction of the Lounge. He is a dapper little man of about twenty-eight. His voice is rather shrill.

ALBERT: Beverley—by God, it *is* you. I was having tea

8

with Violet; she saw you first. This is divine—how are
you?

BEVERLEY: Completely shattered at the moment. We
had a filthy crossing. Do you know Cyril Hardacre?
Albert Hennick.

ALBERT: How are you?

The DAY PORTER *has returned by this time and
gives* BEVERLEY *his change.* BEVERLEY *tips him.*

BEVERLEY: Leave the bags while I go and see about
our rooms. Talk to Cyril for a moment, Albert.

He goes to the Bureau.

ALBERT: I've seen you before somewhere, haven't I?

CYRIL: In London, perhaps.

ALBERT: How long are you staying?

CYRIL: Not long. Beverley wants to go down to
Cannes.

ALBERT: Are you going with him?

CYRIL (*frowning slightly*): Yes.

ALBERT: My dear, how marvellous! You must both
come to a party a friend of mine is giving on Thursday—
Nicco Benelli—d'you know him?

CYRIL: No. I'm afraid I don't.

ALBERT: He's completely mad—you'll love him. Ital-
ian you know—dark and flashy eyes and plays the piano
like an angel. Eric Burnett always says—D'you know
Eric?

CYRIL: No.

ALBERT (*giggling*): Well, you will soon – he's terribly
funny.

BEVERLEY *rejoins them.*

BEVERLEY: We're on the Rue Gilon side.

ALBERT: You must talk to Violet on the way through.
She's dying to see you.

9

BEVERLEY: All right. (*To the* DAY PORTER.) Have the bags sent over as soon as possible.

DAY PORTER: Yes, sir.

BEVERLEY: Come along.

    CYRIL *walks off a few paces in front.*

ALBERT (*to* BEVERLEY *as they go off*): My dear— where did you find that? It's divine!

    Three people—two women and a man walk in from the lounge and——

    out through the swing doors talking as they go.

    As they go out, OWEN MARSHALL *comes in. He is a good-looking man of about thirty. The* DAY PORTER *intercepts him.*

DAY PORTER: Madame is in there, sir—writing letters.

OWEN: Oh, is she? Thanks. (*He comes forward and sees* TANIS.)

TANIS: Hallo, dear. You've been ages!

OWEN (*glancing at his watch*): Three-quarters of an hour.

TANIS: It seemed ages.

OWEN: I was engaged upon a very noble mission.

TANIS: What?

OWEN: Buying you a present.

TANIS: Oh, darling, you shouldn't have. What is it?

OWEN: Here. (*He flings down on the desk a small package.*) I'm giving it to you carelessly as though it meant nothing.

TANIS (*playing up*): It's such a bore receiving presents—can't you wait until I'm less busy.

OWEN: Open it for God's sake. (*He gives a cautious look around and kisses the back of her neck.*)

    She proceeds to open the package. During the whole of the ensuing scene various people arrive

*with luggage, etc., or pass out through the swing
doors. One fails to catch their conversation, being so
completely engrossed in* TANIS *and* OWEN.

TANIS (*disclosing small box*): "Cartier"! Oh, darling!

OWEN: I felt the moment had come for a *"beau
geste"*.

TANIS *opens the box and takes out an exquisite
little cigarette case.*

TANIS: Owen!

OWEN: Do you like it?

TANIS: Like it? It's heavenly; it's perfect——

OWEN: I saw it in the window—leering at me.

TANIS: I can't begin to tell you how I love it—and
you.

She gives a swift glance round, then draws his
head down and kisses him.

OWEN: I suppose I should have waited until we were
in our room to give it to you.

TANIS (*smiling*): Yes—you should have, really.

OWEN: I couldn't.

TANIS: It's going to stay here out of its box right by
me—while I finish these postcards.

OWEN: It's frightful of you to write postcards on a
honeymoon.

TANIS: You'd better send some too.

OWEN: Heaven forbid.

TANIS: Do—there's a darling—send one to George
from us both—and Freda. They're on my mind.

OWEN: Oh, all right. (*He sits down opposite her.*)

TANIS: You only need say, "Here we are in Paris."

OWEN: They know that already.

TANIS: Never mind—they'll love to be sure of it.

While they are both concentrating on their writing

INEZ ZULIETA *and* CYNTHIA GABLE *come through
the swing doors.* INEZ *is slightly older than* CYNTHIA.
*They are both dressed with rather affected simplic-
ity.*

INEZ (*coming forward and sitting by the table*): I'll
wait here.

CYNTHIA: Don't be so silly.

INEZ: I'll be quite happy. You needn't worry about
me. (*She assumes a martyred expression.*)

CYNTHIA: I do wish you wouldn't be so difficult.

TANIS (*looking up at* OWEN): The Bath Club will find
Philip, won't it?

OWEN: Yes. They'll forward it on, anyhow.

INEZ: I'm not being in the least difficult.

CYNTHIA: There are moments when you're infuri-
ating.

INEZ: Thank you.

CYNTHIA (*lowering her voice*): What is there to be
jealous about?

INEZ: Everything—you don't know her like I do.

CYNTHIA (*sharply*): That's true enough.

INEZ: Why say things like that?

CYNTHIA: Well, you told me yourself.

INEZ: That was all over years ago.

CYNTHIA: I didn't say it wasn't.

INEZ: You're damnably cruel sometimes.

CYNTHIA: Why don't you trust me?

INEZ: Trust you——

CYNTHIA: Yes; I feel as though I were in a cage.

INEZ: Cynthia darling——

CYNTHIA: What?

INEZ: I do trust you—really—but don't go and see
her now.

CYNTHIA: Why not?

INEZ: You know perfectly well.

CYNTHIA: Just because you've worked yourself up into a ridiculous state . . .

INEZ: I haven't done anything of the sort.

CYNTHIA: You have.

INEZ: I wish you'd give me back my pride.

CYNTHIA: Don't be melodramatic.

INEZ: And with it the courage never to see you again.
She gets up abruptly and goes out.

CYNTHIA (*following her*): Inez—Inez——
She goes out after her.

OWEN (*blotting a postcard and sitting back*): I've got seats for the Guitrys.

TANIS: Grand! I love them.

OWEN: You're really awfully nice to go on a honeymoon with—so appreciative.

TANIS: I'm intensely happy.

OWEN: Are you—honestly?

TANIS: Can't you see?

OWEN: Yes, I suppose so. I never thought I should be able to get away with it.

TANIS: What?

OWEN: Making you happy.

TANIS: Neither did I—at first.

OWEN (*almost hurt*): Tanis!

TANIS (*gently*): I love you now, you know—that makes all the difference.

OWEN: And you didn't before?

TANIS (*looking down*): No. I felt awfully ashamed—marrying you.

OWEN (*definitely hurt—leaning towards her*): I don't understand.

TANIS: I liked you.

OWEN (*with faint sarcasm*): I'm very glad, I'm sure.

TANIS: Don't be cross, darling. It really is all right now.

OWEN: Is it?

TANIS: It's frightfully difficult to love people right away, you know.

OWEN: I never found it difficult with you.

TANIS: I was very grateful to you for that.

OWEN: Dear—what are you talking about?

TANIS: Nothing particular. I feel amazingly free and content and I just wanted to explain why.

OWEN: Explain away then.

TANIS: No—not now—this is neither the time or the place.

OWEN: Is there anything on your mind?

TANIS: No, darling, and even the things that were are rapidly sliding off.

OWEN: Oh, darling!

TANIS: Well?

OWEN: I'm afraid you're being a little tiresome.

TANIS: I know—maddening. Please forgive me.

OWEN (*rising*): I suppose we'd better go up and dress.

TANIS: And linger over it.

OWEN: You always do.

TANIS: Darling. (*She pinches his arm.*)

OWEN (*picking up a postcard*): You've forgotten a beautiful bird's-eye view of Versailles. (*He turns it over.*) I didn't know you knew Benny Jowett.

TANIS: That's the last postcard I shall ever send him.

OWEN: Why?

TANIS (*sighing*): Oh dear!

OWEN: What on earth is the matter with you to-day?

TANIS: I'm going to be awfully true to you. I've got a tremendous ideal about it.

OWEN: I can't begin to imagine not being true to you.

TANIS (*with utter sincerity*): I love you so very deeply.

OWEN: Sweetheart! (*He kisses her.*)

TANIS (*taking his arm*): Darling—I'm sure that woman saw us!

They go out, pausing at the entrance to the lounge to allow a group of people to pass on their way out.

CURTAIN SLOWLY FALLS

ACT I

SCENE II

TIME: *A few days after Scene I. Just before lunch.*

SCENE: *The communicating passage-way between the Place du Cœur and the Rue Gilon side. There are several show-cases exhibiting clothes, jewellery, perfume, etc., standing at equal distances from one another.*

Apart from the individual characters in the play, other people pass back and forth. There is a kiosk of magazines and papers a little to the R., a GIRL *in black is in charge of it, seated on a stool by the side. When the curtain rises, the stage is empty with the exception of the* GIRL. *A man, dapperly dressed,*

walks rapidly across from R. to L. He is obviously in
a hurry and might almost be French.
MARION FAWCETT *enters from L. She is somewhere*
between thirty and forty and dressed smartly. She
has almost reached the kiosk when INEZ *and*
CYNTHIA *enter from R.*

MARION: Hallo, Inez. How are you?
INEZ: Exhausted, dear. You know Cynthia, don't
you?
MARION: Of course. (*She shakes hands with* CYN-
THIA.) You haven't seen a dark little American girl with a
sort of wood-violet face loitering about, have you?
INEZ: Yes, hundreds.
MARION: Gloria Craig gave her a letter of introduc-
tion to me. I must find her and give her lunch.
CYNTHIA: Well, if you don't succeed, come and lunch
with us.
INEZ: I'm not lunching.
CYNTHIA (*warningly*): Inez!
INEZ: I have to go to Chanel's.
CYNTHIA (*to* MARION): Well, lunch with *me* then. I'll
be in the Restaurant.
MARION: Thanks, my dear. See you later, Inez.
　　She goes off.
INEZ (*as they walk across*): I suppose it's too much to
expect that you should ever wish to lunch with me
alone.
CYNTHIA: Don't be ridiculous.
INEZ: I'm not ridiculous. You know I loathe Marion
Fawcett.
CYNTHIA: I don't know anything of the sort.
INEZ (*angrily*): Go and lunch with her then—lunch

and dine and sup with all the people I hate most—
and discuss me with them and break up everything.

CYNTHIA (*quickly*): I will—if you're not careful!

> *As they are about to go off*—CYRIL *walks on L.*

CYRIL: Oh, how do you do?

INEZ (*shaking hands*): I'd no idea you were in Paris.

CYRIL: I'm over here with Beverley.

INEZ: My dear boy, how unoriginal.

CYRIL: Is it?

INEZ: How's Francis?

CYRIL: Oh, all right, I think.

INEZ: Give him my love when you see him.

CYRIL: Certainly I will. Good-bye. (*He bows and
walks on.*)

> *They go off.*

> JEROME KENNEDY *and* NORMA *enter from R.*
> JEROME *is about forty, slightly grey-haired and
> distinctly attractive.* NORMA *is about eighteen—fair
> and slim and self-assured.*

CYRIL: Did you say Restaurant or Grill?

JEROME: Restaurant.

NORMA: I thought you'd muddle it.

CYRIL: I say—I'm most awfully sorry.

JEROME: Have you been waiting long?

CYRIL: About twenty minutes.

JEROME: We'll go to the Grill, the Restaurant's teem-
ing with angry women.

NORMA: Oh no, Father.

JEROME: Well, we'll see what it looks like anyhow.

> *They stroll across towards L.*

> ALBERT *and* BEVERLEY *enter from L.*

BEVERLEY (*to* CYRIL): Hallo.

CYRIL (*irritably*): Oh, hallo.

ALBERT *and* BEVERLEY *pass on.*

The KENNEDYS *and* CYRIL *stroll off.*

ALBERT (*just as they are nearly off*): Have you been having a row?

BEVERLEY: Good-looking people are always difficult to manage.

ALBERT (*giggling*): You're right. We are.

BEVERLEY (*to* GIRL *at kiosk*): Have you got *Vanity Fair*?

GIRL: Oui, monsieur. (*She hands it to him.*)

BEVERLEY (*paying her for it*): Here.

GIRL: Merci, monsieur.

ALBERT: Do get *La Vie Parisienne*, it's so defiantly normal!

BEVERLEY: Be quiet, Albert.

They go off.

The stage is empty for a moment. DOROTHY *and* JULIUS *stroll on from R., pausing in front of show-cases.* JULIUS LEVENOVITCH *is a tall, good-looking slightly over-dressed Russian.*

DOROTHY: And didn't they give you any food?

JULIUS: Just black bread every day or so. One did not feel like eating much.

DOROTHY: I understand.

JULIUS: I know you do.

DOROTHY: It seems so unfair that people should have to suffer so much.

JULIUS: Perhaps I deserved it. Who knows.

DOROTHY: You must teach me Russian.

JULIUS: I would love to.

DOROTHY: I know just a few words already.

JULIUS: What are they?

DOROTHY (*smiling*): I can't tell you now.

JULIUS: Why not?

DOROTHY: I don't know you well enough. (*At show-case.*) Do look at that frock. Isn't it frightful?

JULIUS: Are you staying here long?

DOROTHY: Only a few days. We're going to Cannes.

JULIUS: We?

DOROTHY: Suzanne and me—and Mike.

JULIUS: That short man you were dining with last night?

DOROTHY: Yes, Mike Craven. You must meet him.

JULIUS: Must I?

DOROTHY (*laughing*): You really are terrible.

> *They go off.*
>
> CYNTHIA *walks on from L.* ELISE TRENT *enters at the same moment from R. They exchange a long look and* ELISE *passes on.* MARION *enters from R. with* BERYL. *They are talking gaily.*

CYNTHIA: You found her all right then?

MARION: Yes. Beryl Fletcher—Cynthia Gable.

CYNTHIA: How d'you do.

BERYL: I'm so pleased to meet you. I know you by sight.

CYNTHIA: How nice of you.

MARION: Where's Inez?

CYNTHIA: She stamped out into the Rue Gilon.

MARION (*laughing*): You are divine, Cynthia.

CYNTHIA: I'm very cross.

MARION: Come and lunch with us in the Grill.

CYNTHIA: I asked you to lunch with me if you didn't find Miss Fletcher.

MARION: Well, let's all lunch with each other.

CYNTHIA: All right.

BERYL (*as they go off*): I'm coming over by myself in the Fall to learn French properly.

They all three go off L.

OWEN and TANIS come in from R. TANIS stops at kiosk.

TANIS: Let's stop and load up with magazines for the train.

OWEN: All right.

The KENNEDYS enter from L. with CYRIL.

JEROME: Why don't you come South with us?

CYRIL: God, I should love it, but——

NORMA: Anyhow, we shall see you somewhere about, shan't we?

CYRIL: Yes—oh yes.

Just as they are passing the kiosk TANIS turns to JEROME, thinking it is OWEN.

TANIS (*brandishing the sketch*): Darling, do look at this awful photograph of Sylvia. (*Realising her mistake.*) Oh, I beg your pardon.

JEROME (*smiling*): Not at all.

He and NORMA and CYRIL exit. NORMA laughs.

TANIS: Owen, I'm covered in shame. I've called a perfectly strange man "Darling"!

CURTAIN

ACT I

Scene III

TIME: *March. Before lunch.*

SCENE: *The Bar on the Rue Gilon side. It is a small compact room with entrance back C., facing the entrance to the Men's Bar. There are small tables round the walls and dishes of olives and crisp potato flakes on each table.*

There is a group of three people sitting at a table L. upstage. They are drinking cocktails and talking in undertones. Their conversation is inaudible, being immaterial to the action of the play.

CYRIL HARDACRE enters, looks round and sits at table R. A WAITER comes in with fresh cocktails for the people L. After he has delivered them CYRIL calls him.

CYRIL: Garçon.

WAITER: Monsieur?

CYRIL: Two Martinis with a dash.

WAITER: Bien, monsieur.

CYRIL: Make one of them double.

WAITER: Oui, monsieur.

The WAITER departs.

CYRIL looks at his wrist watch and lights a cigarette. DOROTHY PRICE and SUZANNE FELLINI enter and seat themselves at table down L.

SUZANNE: I think you're an awful fool to do this.

DOROTHY: Oh, shut up, Suzanne.

SUZANNE: Well, I do.

DOROTHY: There's no harm in lunch, is there?

SUZANNE: A good deal, I should imagine.

DOROTHY: That's your dirty mind, dear.

SUZANNE: Thanks.

DOROTHY: I don't intend to be a slave to anyone ever.

SUZANNE: Slaves don't get as much out of life as you do.

DOROTHY: Mike doesn't arrive until this evening anyhow.

SUZANNE: He might fly over.

DOROTHY: Not he—he'd be too frightened of getting into an air pocket.

SUZANNE: Your passion for intrigue will wreck you one day.

DOROTHY: Don't croak.

SUZANNE: It wrecked me.

DOROTHY: That was different—you weren't discreet.

SUZANNE: I thought I was.

DOROTHY: My dear, Mike is far too conceited to imagine anyone could be unfaithful to him.

SUZANNE: Are you sure?

DOROTHY: Anyhow I haven't been—yet.

SUZANNE: He's no fool really, you know.

DOROTHY: He is over me.

SUZANNE: You're so sure of yourself.

DOROTHY (exasperated): Now look here, Suzanne— I'm merely lunching here with you and Julius.

SUZANNE: No, dear—you're merely lunching here with Julius.

DOROTHY: How's Mike to know that?

SUZANNE: Here's the waiter.

The WAITER *has returned with* CYRIL'S *cocktails which he places on the table.* CYRIL *pays him.*

The three people upstage L. get up and go out.

DOROTHY: Garçon.

WAITER: Oui, madame.

DOROTHY: One Bronx—what do you want, Suzanne?

SUZANNE: Porto Flip.

DOROTHY: How disgusting! (*To* WAITER.) And one Porto Flip.

SUZANNE: And bring some more of these potatoes, will you.

WAITER: Bien, madame.

He takes empty potato dish and goes off.

SUZANNE: Do you honestly think Julius is worth all this trouble?

DOROTHY: There hasn't been any trouble.

SUZANNE: There will be.

DOROTHY (*with sarcasm*): You're being *such* a comfort, dear.

SUZANNE: I've known Mike longer than you have.

DOROTHY: Yes, but not so intimately.

SUZANNE: Exactly—one can see better when one's not too close.

DOROTHY: You've got a hangover this morning. That's what it is.

SUZANNE: Why not wait until Mike goes away?

DOROTHY: I'll be an old woman before he does that— he keeps putting it off—putting it off——

SUZANNE: Has it ever struck you that he's pretty deeply in love with you?

DOROTHY: Don't, dear, you're breaking my heart.

SUZANNE: And I think making a fool of him after all you got from him is not only dangerous but rather second-rate.

DOROTHY: Now look here, Suzanne.

23

SUZANNE: I mean it.

DOROTHY: To hear you talk anyone would think I was never out of bed with Julius.

SUZANNE: He's nothing but a cheap little Russian pimp, anyhow!

DOROTHY (*furious*): How dare you say that!

SUZANNE: The nearest he ever got to the old nobility was seeing their pictures in the *Daily Mirror*.

DOROTHY: You're jealous—anyone could see that.

SUZANNE: Jealous! That's funny!

DOROTHY: I think it's pathetic.

SUZANNE (*rising*): You self-satisfied little fool—you can manage your own filthy intrigues—I'm not going to be mixed up in them.

DOROTHY (*acidly*): Aren't you going to wait for your Porto Flip, darling?

SUZANNE (*irately*): You know what you can do with that, don't you?

DOROTHY: Oh, go to hell!

> SUZANNE *stalks out—nearly banging into——*
> NORMA *who is coming in.* CYRIL *rises.*

NORMA: Am I terribly late?

CYRIL: No, not a bit—I was early.

NORMA: I've been shopping.

CYRIL: Here's a cocktail for you.

NORMA (*sitting down and loosening her furs*): Thank God.

CYRIL: When are you going back to London?

NORMA: To-morrow—or the day after.

CYRIL (*despondently*): Oh!

NORMA: Don't look so gloomy.

CYRIL: I can't help it.

NORMA: Cyril dear—you mustn't be silly, you know.

24

CYRIL: I'm not silly.

NORMA: You are—a little.

CYRIL: You were much nicer to me in Cannes.

NORMA: Was I?

CYRIL: You know you were.

NORMA: How's your singing going?

CYRIL: Damn my singing!

NORMA: Are you working hard?

CYRIL: Yes—far too hard.

NORMA: How's Beverley Ford?

CYRIL: I don't know—I haven't seen him since Cannes.

NORMA: I'm glad of that.

CYRIL: Why?

NORMA: I'm not a fool, Cyril.

CYRIL: I don't know what you mean.

NORMA: Yes, you do—perfectly well.

CYRIL: I wish you wouldn't insinuate things.

NORMA (*lightly*): You forget, dear, that apart from being an extremely bright modern young girl, I happen to be the daughter of a novelist—life holds out no surprises for me. I'm occasionally pained but never shocked.

CYRIL: Oh God!

NORMA: What's the matter?

CYRIL: You frighten me.

NORMA: Don't be ingenuous, Cyril, or you'll arouse the maternal in me.

CYRIL: I love you.

NORMA (*gently*): Shut up.

CYRIL: Why should I?

NORMA: Because as I've told you before—it's no use.

CYRIL: I suppose you were only sweet to me in Cannes, because you felt I needed reforming.

NORMA: I certainly felt that you were on the wrong track.

CYRIL: And you didn't care for me at all?

NORMA: Of course I did—I do now—I think you're a dear.

CYRIL: I see.

NORMA: I'm afraid you don't.

CYRIL: Are you in love with anyone else?

NORMA: No.

CYRIL: Honestly!

NORMA (*with faint hesitation*): I don't think so.

CYRIL: I suppose you don't want to lunch with me.

NORMA: Yes, I do—very much.

CYRIL: I'm not going to be very gay or amusing.

NORMA: I don't want you to be.

CYRIL: I'm utterly miserable.

NORMA: Look here, Cyril—don't be weak and self-pitying. I'm not going to be false and play up to you. I respect you too much.

CYRIL (*contemptuously*): Respect!

NORMA: Yes—and you're wrong about me trying to reform you—I wouldn't try to reform anybody—I realised in Cannes that you were in quite the wrong métier and not particularly happy in it. It's awfully difficult to find one's level these days—nothing matters really except being sure of what you want—and you weren't.

CYRIL: I am now—and I'm more wretched than I've ever been in my life.

NORMA: You'll get over that—and anyhow you do *know* about yourself.

The WAITER *comes in with a cocktail and Porto Flip for* DOROTHY.

DOROTHY: I don't want the Porto Flip after all—will you take it back?

WAITER: Oui, madam.

DOROTHY (*paying him*): Here.

WAITER: Merci, madame.

CYRIL: Do you want another cocktail?

NORMA: No, thanks.

CYRIL: I think I do.

NORMA: You've already had a double one.

CYRIL: Oh, all right—let's go and have lunch.

They get up to go and meet JEROME *coming in. Two people come in after him and sit at a table up stage R.*

NORMA: Hallo, Father!

JEROME: Hallo. (*He shakes hands with* CYRIL.) Are you two lunching here?

CYRIL: Yes.

JEROME: It's all right. Don't look scared, Cyril. I don't intend to join you. I'm lunching with the Marshalls.

NORMA: The Marshalls?

JEROME: Yes, you remember that woman in Cannes who played tennis with us—and her husband?

NORMA: Oh yes—I remember.

JEROME: We're dining at 7.30, remember—so don't be late.

NORMA: Don't fuss, dear—I'll be there.

JEROME (*to* CYRIL): Good-bye, young man.

CYRIL: Good-bye.

JEROME: Look us up if you come over to London.

CYRIL: Thanks awfully—I will.

Goes out with NORMA.

Jerome goes and sits at the table they've just left. He rings the bell for the WAITER *and lights a cigarette.* CYNTHIA *and* ELISE *enter and sit at a table just below* DOROTHY.

ELISE: They did the whole thing with masks.

CYNTHIA: Marvellous!

ELISE: I really feel that they're getting somewhere, you know.

CYNTHIA: Inez doesn't—she resents anything progressive in opera.

ELISE: Naturally—she still clings to the old school.

The WAITER *enters and goes over to* JEROME—*his ensuing dialogue with the* WAITER *and* CYNTHIA *and* ELISE *should be spoken simultaneously.*

JEROME: Garçon.

WAITER: Monsieur?

JEROME: Bring me a double Manhattan.

WAITER: Oui, monsieur.

JEROME: And some Turkish cigarettes.

WAITER: Abdullah, monsieur?

JEROME: Yes, they'll do—bring them quickly.

WAITER: Tout de suite, monsieur.

ELISE: What do you want, dear?

CYNTHIA: I don't care.

ELISE: Stingers are delicious.

CYNTHIA: Stingers?

ELISE: Yes, very potent—crème de menthe and brandy.

CYNTHIA: We shall be under the table.

ELISE: Never mind; we ought to celebrate really.

CYNTHIA: Darling. (*She squeezes* ELISE'S *hand under the table.*)

28

ELISE: Garçon.

WAITER: Madame?

ELISE: Two Stingers.

WAITER: Bien, madame.

He goes off.

DOROTHY *rises from her table with slight irritability and goes and stands just outside the door waiting.*

ELISE: Does Inez know—d'you think?

CYNTHIA: I can't help it if she does.

ELISE: But does she?

CYNTHIA: She suspects.

ELISE: I shouldn't think that was anything new.

CYNTHIA: You're right—it isn't.

ELISE: I can't imagine how you've stood it for so long.

CYNTHIA: Neither can I—now.

ELISE: Will she make a scene?

CYNTHIA: I expect so.

ELISE: You don't seem to mind much.

CYNTHIA: I'm used to them.

ELISE: Poor Inez.

CYNTHIA: It serves her right really—she's always so untrusting.

ELISE (*laughing*): Darling—that's funny!

CYNTHIA (*laughing too*): Yes, I suppose it is rather.

ELISE: I feel a bit guilty.

CYNTHIA: Why?

ELISE: It was my fault in the first place.

CYNTHIA: No, it wasn't. I saw you before you ever saw me.

ELISE: Where?

CYNTHIA: Philippe's about two years ago—dining with a red-haired woman.

ELISE: Nadia Balaishieff.

CYNTHIA: Where is she now?

ELISE: New York, I think. I really don't know.

CYNTHIA: Tell me, Elise—are you as utterly ruthless
as you pretend to be?

ELISE: I don't pretend ever.

CYNTHIA: I'm glad.

ELISE: It's funny you remembering me all that time—
life's made up of circles, isn't it?

CYNTHIA: Perhaps.

ELISE: Are you going to tell Inez?

CYNTHIA: Yes, I suppose so.

ELISE: When?

CYNTHIA: I don't know.

ELISE: Soon?

CYNTHIA: She's bound to know—very soon indeed.

ELISE: Why don't you get it over at once?

CYNTHIA: The opportunity will occur of its own
accord.

ELISE: That's rather cowardly of you.

CYNTHIA: She's got to go to Dresden next month
anyhow.

ELISE: Will you come to me then?

CYNTHIA: Yes.

ELISE: Next month—it's a long way ahead.

> The WAITER *appears with their cocktails*, ELISE
> *pays him.*

WAITER: Merci, madame.

> The WAITER *delivers* JEROME'S *cocktail and ciga-*
> *rettes.*

CYNTHIA (*sipping her drink*): This is delicious.

ELISE: They're awfully easy to make.

> INEZ *enters wrapped in furs and looking*

extremely sullen—she sees them and approaches the table.

(*Affably.*) Good morning, Inez.

INEZ (*ignoring her—to* CYNTHIA): I want to speak to you.

ELISE (*half rising*): Shall I go?

CYNTHIA: Certainly not—stay where you are.

INEZ: I should like you to go, please.

CYNTHIA: Don't be a fool, Inez.

ELISE: This is very embarrassing.

INEZ: I'm surprised that you find it so—it's a situation you must be well accustomed to.

ELISE: I shouldn't raise your voice quite so much if I were you—it's rather silly.

INEZ: Mind your own business.

CYNTHIA: Inez!

INEZ: You've lied to me.

CYNTHIA: You're behaving fantastically.

INEZ: Will you go back to the flat sometime during the afternoon and pack your things.

CYNTHIA (*rising, furiously*): How dare you!

ELISE (*pulling her down*): Ssh, Cynthia.

INEZ (*softly*): I hate you—I hate you—I hate you!
        She walks out.

CYNTHIA (*after a pause—shuddering*): How horrible!

ELISE: Are you going after her?

CYNTHIA: No.

ELISE: Good! (*She finishes her drink.*)

CYNTHIA: How dare she talk to me like that—how dare she! (*She breaks into tears.*)

ELISE: Cynthia—for heaven's sake—don't be an idiot. (*She presses her arm.*)

CYNTHIA: Don't touch me.

31

ELISE: Darling, pull yourself together.

CYNTHIA: Let's go quickly—quickly——

ELISE: Very well—come along.

They go out as——

TANIS MARSHALL *comes in.* DOROTHY PRICE *also re-enters and returns to her table.* TANIS *sees* JEROME.

TANIS: I've been waiting for Owen over at the other side but I left a message with the porter.

JEROME: Good. D'you want a cocktail?

TANIS (*sitting down*): No, thanks—you'd better order for Owen.

JEROME *rings bell for* WAITER.

JEROME: It's awfully nice seeing you again.

TANIS: I'm feeling awfully homesick for the South—all that lovely sunshine and everything.

JEROME: It was divine, wasn't it?

TANIS: When do you go back to London?

JEROME: The day after to-morrow, I think.

TANIS: So are we—we shall meet on the train.

The WAITER *appears.*

JEROME: What do you think your husband would like?

TANIS: Oh, anything—a Martini, I should think.

JEROME: Bring a Martini, will you?

WAITER: Oui, monsieur.

JEROME: Cigarette?

TANIS (*taking one*): Thanks. Are you working on a new book?

JEROME: I shall start directly I get back.

TANIS: You do lead a grand life, don't you?

JEROME: I enjoy myself, I think—on the whole.

TANIS: How's Norma?

32

JEROME: Frightfully well and extremely energetic as usual.

TANIS: She's awfully amusing.

JEROME: They all are—this younger generation.

TANIS: You talk as though you were seventy!

JEROME: It's having a grown-up daughter—I feel seventy sometimes.

TANIS: Your tennis seems still to retain a certain amount of youthful vigour.

JEROME (*laughing*): Thanks.

TANIS (*looking across at* DOROTHY): There's that woman we saw in the Ambassadeur that night.

JEROME: Oh yes—so it is. Wasn't she the one who had a fearful scene with the little red-faced man?

TANIS: Yes—look at her pearls.

JEROME: God bless the little red-faced man!

TANIS: People are amusing, aren't they, to watch?

JEROME: In this atmosphere they rather lack variety.

   The WAITER *brings the cocktail.* JEROME *pays for it.*

TANIS: It's really very tiresome of Owen to be so late.

JEROME: I'm perfectly happy.

TANIS: I should like to have all the money in the world and rush up and down the Rue de la Paix with a barrow.

JEROME: I know that feeling.

   OWEN *enters and approaches them.*

TANIS: Here he is at last.

OWEN: I'm terribly sorry——(*He shakes hands with* JEROME.)

JEROME: It doesn't matter a bit—here's a Martini for you.

OWEN: Thanks—I'll swallow it down in one gulp. (*He does so.*)

TANIS: Where *have* you been?

OWEN: At the bank, dear—hedged in by enthusiastic tourists.

JEROME: Shall we go and lunch?

TANIS (*crushing out her cigarette*): Yes, let's.

JEROME: Come along, then.

TANIS (*as they go out*): Isn't it fun, Owen—Mr. Kennedy is going over to London on Thursday with us.

> *They go out.*
>
> *A group of people enter and sit down.* DOROTHY, *by this time extremely impatient, gathers herself together preparatory to leaving. Finally* JULIUS *enters hurriedly.*

JULIUS: Dorothy!

DOROTHY: I was just going.

JULIUS: Forgive me, please.

DOROTHY: I've been here for hours.

JULIUS: Don't be angry.

DOROTHY: I'm not angry—only bored.

JULIUS: Please smile.

DOROTHY: Why are you so late?

JULIUS: Just one smile.

DOROTHY: You haven't answered me.

JULIUS: There is only one way I could answer you.

DOROTHY: Well, why don't you?

JULIUS: It's too public.

DOROTHY: Now then.

JULIUS: Do you want to lunch here?

DOROTHY: I don't care.

JULIUS: Don't you?

DOROTHY: Not a bit.

JULIUS: You look wonderful.

DOROTHY: Thanks.

JULIUS: I'm glad I was late.

DOROTHY: Why?

JULIUS: Because I've never seen you angry before—I want to know you in every mood.

DOROTHY: I'd begun to think you weren't coming at all.

JULIUS: Where is Suzanne?

DOROTHY: Suzanne's a bloody fool.

JULIUS: I didn't say what is she—I said where is she?

DOROTHY: I don't know and I don't care.

JULIUS: I'm glad you got rid of her.

DOROTHY: Do you want a cocktail?

JULIUS: No thank you. Do you?

DOROTHY: I've had one.

JULIUS: Another?

DOROTHY: No.

JULIUS: Come, then.

DOROTHY: We haven't decided where to go yet.

JULIUS: We'll decide in the taxi.

DOROTHY: I'd rather walk.

JULIUS: Don't be cruel.

DOROTHY: Well, I would—I know about you in taxis.

JULIUS: You haven't smiled yet.

DOROTHY: There——(*She grimaces at him.*)

JULIUS: Beautiful!

DOROTHY: Where are we lunching?

JULIUS: The other side of the river.

DOROTHY: Oh no, we're not.

JULIUS: Yes—please.

DOROTHY: Some awful little café?

JULIUS: No.

DOROTHY: Where then?

JULIUS: No café at all.

DOROTHY: Do you mean——?

JULIUS: Yes, please.

DOROTHY: Well, really—you have got a nerve.

JULIUS: Lunch is all ready—delicious—that's why I was late.

DOROTHY: Suppose I don't come?

JULIUS: I shall throw it all out of the window.

DOROTHY: You are absurd! (*She smiles.*)

JULIUS: The smile—at last——

DOROTHY (*as they go out*): Alone in Paris with an amorous Russian—so help me God!

CURTAIN

ACT II

Scene I

TIME: *January 1925. Just after lunch.*
SCENE: *The lounge—Rue Gilon side. On the right is the exit to the Rue Gilon and entrances to the Bars off stage. To the left down stage, entrance to the Grill Room. French windows up left opening onto terrace. There is a big sofa across middle of stage behind which is entrance to communicating passage far up left and far up right the lifts.*

When the curtain rises four people come out of the Grill Room. The women depart for the Ladies' room and the men to get their hats and coats R. CYRIL enters from communicating passage. He comes down and looks into Grill Room, then goes over to sofa and sits down. The two men return to view, hatted and coated, and wait for the women who presently rejoin them and they all go out together. INEZ enters from R.

INEZ: My dear boy, how can you manage to look so hearty and well after that *fearful* party?
CYRIL (*having risen*): I feel marvellous really—considering.
INEZ: You sang quite beautifully—why did I never know you had a voice like that?
CYRIL (*pleased*): Well, you see, I——

INEZ: Are you studying?

CYRIL: Yes—with Farelli.

INEZ: My dear, you must leave him at once.

CYRIL: Oh—why?

INEZ: He shuts up people's throats like mouse-traps—Look at poor Griselda Menken—the most constipated Carmen I've ever heard.

CYRIL: I thought she was rather good.

INEZ: Why don't you come and have tea with me sometime?

CYRIL: Thanks, most awfully—I'd love to.

INEZ: Do you live in this hotel?

CYRIL: No.

INEZ: Well, you shouldn't loiter about here so much—you'll make people think you do.

CYRIL: Do you think that would be bad for my reputation?

INEZ: I know a good deal more about your reputation than you imagine. I'm afraid you're rather a naughty boy, aren't you?

CYRIL (laughing): In what way?

INEZ: The usual ways.

CYRIL: You know you're quite different from when I met you first—last year.

INEZ: Am I?

CYRIL: Yes—I used to be terrified of you.

INEZ: I was passing through a tiresome phase.

CYRIL: I would like to hear you sing sometime.

INEZ: I'm rehearsing this afternoon for my concert—you can come if you promise to sit quietly and not say a word.

CYRIL: I'd love to—where shall I come?

INEZ: Soixante-sept rue des Saint Pères—five o'clock.

CYRIL: It's awfully sweet of you to let me.

    BEVERLEY FORD *enters from the Grill Room.*

BEVERLEY: Cyril?

CYRIL: Hallo, Beverley.

BEVERLEY: Inez, my dear—you're looking marvellous.

INEZ (*to* CYRIL): Beverley's so insincere—I adore him.

BEVERLEY: Lady Gailby's in the Grill Room wearing a hat like a Directoire wedding cake.

INEZ (*laughing*): Isn't he ridiculous.

BEVERLEY: I couldn't take my eyes off it—Would you like to dine with me tonight, Cyril?

CYRIL: I'm afraid I can't tonight.

INEZ: Lest old acquaintance be forgot!

BEVERLEY: Really, Inez, you're divine—tongue like a scorpion. (*To* CYRIL.) Beware of her, Cyril—she's the most dangerous woman in Paris—prima donnas always know far too much anyhow.

INEZ: None of the ones I've met know anything. I must go now, my dears. I promised to meet Helen Saville in the Restaurant at two o'clock sharp—it's now at least four.

CYRIL (*glancing at his wrist watch*): Twenty-past two to be exact.

INEZ (*patting his arm*): You'll never be a good singer if you're exact in your private life—don't forget, five o'clock. Soixante-sept rue des Saint Pères—Good-bye, Beverley. Do come to my concert.

BEVERLEY: *Nothing* could keep me away.

    INEZ *waves gratefully and goes off in the direction of the communicating passage.*

Inez is so much more amusing when she's not in love.

CYRIL: So is everybody else.

BEVERLEY: I think Cynthia behaved pretty badly all the same.

CYRIL: Oh, do shut up, Beverley!

BEVERLEY: You're becoming far too hearty these days, Cyril. You were awfully rude to Albert the other day—he'll never forgive you.

CYRIL: I don't want him to.

BEVERLEY: Even if you are reverting to the commonplace, surely there's no necessity to be so truculent about it. (*He walks over to get his hat and coat.*)

　　NORMA *enters hurriedly from the Grill Room.*

CYRIL: Norma.

NORMA: Cyril—I haven't seen you for ages.

CYRIL: I know you haven't.

NORMA: How are you?

CYRIL: All right, thanks.

NORMA: Studying hard?

CYRIL: Yes—I told you I was in my letters.

NORMA: Of course you did.

CYRIL: Which you never answered.

NORMA: I'm always terrible about answering letters.

　　There is a slight pause.

CYRIL: I suppose you're not going to be in Paris for long, are you?

NORMA: No—we go to St. Moritz to-morrow.

CYRIL: Oh, I see.

　　There is another pause.

NORMA (*conversationally*): I wish we were staying longer really—I'd rather be in Paris than anywhere.

CYRIL: I wish you were, too.

NORMA: Have you still got your studio?

CYRIL: Yes.

Norma: I'd love to come and see it when we come back.

Cyril: You wouldn't really, you know—you're just being polite.

Norma: Don't be so silly, Cyril.

Cyril: Why don't you say outright that I bore you stiff?—it would be more honest.

Norma: What on earth is the matter with you?

Cyril: Do you think it was quite fair of you to be as nice to me as you were last year and then leave me utterly flat?

Norma: I haven't done anything of the sort.

Cyril: You had such tremendous plans about improving my life.

Norma: Perhaps you don't feel that my tremendous plans were necessary?

Cyril: I did then.

Norma: And you don't now? Is that it?

Cyril: I certainly haven't got much out of it.

Norma: I'm sorry. I thought you had more intelligence.

Cyril: Thank you.

Norma: I must go now—I'm frightfully late.

Cyril (*turning away*): All right—good-bye.

Norma (*relenting a little*): Cyril—please don't be horrid.

Cyril (*with bitterness*): Horrid?

Norma: Yes—I'm sorry I didn't answer your letters or anything—I am honestly.

Cyril: Rot—you don't give a damn.

Norma (*angry*): Cyril!

Cyril: It's perfectly true and you know it—you don't care if I live or die.

41

NORMA: If you feel like that about it, there's nothing more to be said.

CYRIL: There's this to be said—next time you feel the urge to reform someone—don't muddle it up with your own desire to be made love to.

NORMA: How dare you say that!

CYRIL: I suppose you found it amusing to see how far you could make me give myself away to you—Well, you succeeded beautifully.

NORMA: Shut up or I'll never speak to you again.

CYRIL: I should be far happier if you didn't!

He walks off quickly in the direction of the communicating passage.

NORMA *stands looking after him for a moment, then with a slight shrug of her shoulders—goes out R.*

BERYL FLETCHER *and* MARION FAWCETT *enter from Grill Room.* BERYL *has changed perceptibly since her first arrival in Act I. She is smarter and more assured.*

BERYL: I do think you might come too, Marion.

MARION: Certainly not. I don't approve.

BERYL (*laughing*): Harry adores you—he said so the other night.

MARION: It's very sweet of him, I'm sure.

BERYL: We might do a little shopping on the way.

MARION (*patiently*): Will you take one word of advice from me, dear— go easy on the shopping. Harry's never been renowned for his generosity.

BERYL: He's a perfect darling—I won't hear a word against him.

MARION: You won't be able to help it in some quarters.

BERYL: If I hadn't been staying with you I shouldn't have met him anyhow.

MARION: Oh yes, you would—Harry's always on the track of the fresh and ingenuous.

BERYL (*irately*): I'm *not* fresh and ingenuous.

MARION: Not now, dear.

BERYL (*with slightly forced indignation*): Marion, how can you?

MARION: If I had any sense, I'd pack you off home.

BERYL: I wouldn't go. I'm having far too grand a time.

MARION: You're quite incorrigible. What time are you meeting him?

BERYL: He just said—after lunch.

MARION: He would ... I must go now. I'll be in about six.

BERYL: I doubt if I shall.

MARION: You must—we're dining early.

BERYL (*laughing*): All right, dear. I'll try.

> MARION *goes off up L.*
>
> BERYL *sits down on the sofa and lights a cigarette.*
> DOROTHY PRICE *and* MIKE CRAVEN *come out of the Grill Room quarrelling and go up back R. to the lifts.*

DOROTHY: Oh, for God's sake shut up about it.

MIKE: The next time I hear anything like that there's going to be trouble.

DOROTHY: I don't care.

MIKE: You will.

DOROTHY: Who do you think you are anyway—Pontius Pilate?

> *They pass out of earshot and eventually disappear into the lift.*
>
> HARRY LEFTWICH *enters from direction of street.*

43

He is excellently dressed and about forty-five—nice-
looking in a fulsome way.

HARRY: Beryl!

BERYL: Hallo!

HARRY: You're smoking again—that's awfully
naughty.

BERYL: I had to do something while I was waiting for
you.

HARRY: Have you been waiting long?

BERYL: About half an hour.

HARRY: Where's Marion?

BERYL: I don't know. I haven't seen her since this
morning.

HARRY: I thought you were lunching with her.

BERYL: Oh no, I was lunching with someone else.

HARRY: Who?

BERYL: Let's go now—shall we?

HARRY: Who were you lunching with?

BERYL: Don't be so inquisitive.

HARRY: Why should you try to hide it from me?

BERYL: I'm not trying to hide anything—if you must
know, it was a boy I met coming over on the boat last
year.

HARRY: Have I ever seen him?

BERYL: I don't know—he's tall and fair and rather
athletic-looking.

HARRY: What's his name?

BERYL: Why should you want to know?

HARRY: I don't particularly—come along, my child.

BERYL: I'm not your child.

HARRY: Aren't you?

BERYL: His name's Leo Williams.

HARRY: You've got too much lip rouge on.

44

BERYL (*pursing up her lips at him*): I think it looks rather nice.

HARRY: It's unnecessary.

BERYL (*sweetly*): Are you mad at me?

HARRY: You're spoiling yourself.

BERYL: That's funny coming from you.

HARRY: What do you mean?

BERYL: You know quite well what I mean.

HARRY (*handing her his handkerchief*): Wipe it off.

BERYL (*smiling*): You *do* frighten me, Harry. (*She wipes her lips.*) Is that better? (*She holds her face towards him.*)

HARRY: Much—darling. (*He is about to kiss her when——*)

> A group of people come out of the Grill Room and——
> Walk off R. talking.

BERYL: Here's your handkerchief. (*She gives it to him.*)

HARRY (*pressing it to his lips*): That's for you.

BERYL (*enraptured*): Oh, Harry!

HARRY: Come along now.

BERYL: Where are we going?

HARRY: We'll decide in the car—it's outside.

BERYL: Let's stop for a moment at Coty's.

HARRY: Why?

BERYL: I must get some perfume.

HARRY: You don't want to use scent at your age.

BERYL: Yes, I do.

HARRY: Oh, very well.

BERYL: I think Marion suspects about us.

HARRY (*sharply*): What!

BERYL: Don't look so scared—what does it matter?

Enter GEORGE HUDD *from back L. He is a thick-
     set stocky man.*

GEORGE: Hallo, Harry.

HARRY (*irritably*): Hallo, George.

GEORGE: I've just got in from Holland.

HARRY: Really?

GEORGE: I pulled off a pretty big deal. (*He looks at*
BERYL, *obviously anxious to be introduced.*)

HARRY: That's splendid. (*Grudgingly.*) Miss Fletcher—
Mr. Hudd.

GEORGE (*shaking hands*): How do you do?

BERYL (*with great charm*): I'm so pleased to meet
you.

GEORGE: Didn't I see you at Ciro's one night last
week?

BERYL: Perhaps you did—I often go there.

GEORGE: I'm going to be here for a few days,
Harry—can't we get up a nice little party?

HARRY: I'm rather off parties, George.

GEORGE: You're getting old—that's what it is—eh,
Miss Fletcher? (*He laughs.*)

     DOROTHY *comes out of the lift and advances
     towards them followed by* MIKE. *They are both
     apparently in better tempers.*

DOROTHY: George! Fancy seeing you. I thought you
were in America?

GEORGE (*shaking hands*): No. I've put off going until
May. Hallo, Mike. (*They shake hands.*) Do you know
Miss Fletcher?

MIKE (*shaking hands with* BERYL): How are you?

BERYL: I'm awfully pleased to meet you.

DOROTHY: I've got a message for you, Harry, from
Hazel Clark.

HARRY: Oh, really? I haven't seen her for ages.

DOROTHY: Yes—that was the message—she's furious with you.

GEORGE: Miss Fletcher—Miss Price.

DOROTHY: How do you do—I know you very well by sight.

BERYL: I know you too.

GEORGE: I've been trying to make Harry get up a little party with me.

DOROTHY: Oh yes—when?

GEORGE: What about Thursday?

DOROTHY: That'll be lovely, won't it, Mike? We can have it in our suite.

MIKE: I shan't be here on Thursday.

DOROTHY: Stay over till Friday.

MIKE: I can't.

GEORGE: Make it Wednesday then.

MIKE: Oh, all right.

GEORGE: Does that suit you, Miss Fletcher?

BERYL: I didn't know I was asked.

DOROTHY: Of course you are.

BERYL: How gorgeous—Harry will bring me—won't you, Harry?

HARRY (*without enthusiasm*): Yes, if you like.

GEORGE: Well, that's settled. About 11.30.

DOROTHY: Number 517.

HARRY: All right. Come along, Beryl, we must go.

BERYL (*with a ravishing smile at everybody*): Thanks ever so much.

HARRY: Good-bye, Dorothy.

    He and BERYL *go off.*

GEORGE: Who is that girl?

DOROTHY: I don't know—apart from being Harry's latest.

MIKE: He does like 'em young.

DOROTHY: She's pretty in a funny sort of way.

> JULIUS *enters, bows politely to* DOROTHY *and sits down in an armchair left.*

MIKE (*as he and* GEORGE *and* DOROTHY *walk off*): Who's that man?

DOROTHY: A friend of Suzanne's. Russian I think.

GEORGE: Can I drop you anywhere?

> *They go off talking R.*

> TANIS *and* JEROME *enter from Grill Room.*

TANIS: Jerry dear, I *have* enjoyed my nice lunch.

JEROME: So have I.

TANIS: Don't trouble to wait with me—Owen will be here soon.

JEROME: I shall certainly wait.

TANIS: I'll just go and collect my rich fur coat.

JEROME: All right.

> *She goes off to cloakroom.*

> JEROME *walks over to windows left and stands looking out.* DOROTHY *re-enters hurriedly,* JULIUS *rises.*

DOROTHY (*furtively*): I can't manage this afternoon.

JULIUS: You promised.

DOROTHY: I know—but I can't—I'll call you up this evening.

JULIUS: I must see you—I told you why.

DOROTHY: Haven't you heard from them yet?

JULIUS: No—it's awful.

DOROTHY: Poor old darling—I'll see what I can do this afternoon.

JULIUS: I do hate bothering you, dear.

48

DOROTHY: Don't be silly—Mike may have to dine out to-night.

JULIUS: You will call me up?

DOROTHY: Yes, about six.

JULIUS: Promise?

DOROTHY: Promise—I must fly now—I said I'd left my bag.

JULIUS: You are an angel.

DOROTHY (*putting her finger to her lips*): Shhh!

> *She goes out again quickly.*
>
> TANIS *comes out of the cloakroom.* JEROME *comes down from the windows and meets her.* JULIUS *bites his lip in obvious annoyance and goes out up stage L.* JEROME *and* TANIS *sit on sofa.*

JEROME: Would you like a cigarette?

TANIS: No, thanks. I smoked far too many at lunch.

JEROME: I wish you were coming to Switzerland instead of Italy.

TANIS: So do I.

JEROME: Winter sports are divine.

TANIS: We're rather making conversation, you know.

JEROME: Yes—we are, I'm afraid.

TANIS: Why?

JEROME: I still feel a little dazzled.

TANIS: Dazzled?

JEROME: Yes—lunch was wonderfully illuminating.

TANIS: You mean I've talked too much.

JEROME: Perhaps—in a way.

TANIS: Oh, Jerry—why did you let me?

JEROME: I was fascinated.

TANIS: Life is awfully complicated, isn't it, at moments?

JEROME: Only at moments.

TANIS: No—all the time, really.

JEROME: I feel terribly guilty.

TANIS: Why should you?

JEROME: It's my fault.

TANIS: No—no it isn't.

JEROME: But I don't think I could have helped myself.

TANIS: People change so strangely as one gets to know them better. When we first met I saw you only as a sort of celebrity—nice and rather glamorous.

JEROME: And now the glamour has departed?

TANIS: Yes—that side of it.

JEROME: When did it go?

TANIS: London, I think—when you and Norma came and dined that night. I suddenly found you were a real person.

JEROME: Were you glad?

TANIS: Yes—but rather scared.

JEROME: My dear.

TANIS: Lunch has been illuminating for me, too.

JEROME: Has it really?

TANIS (*looking down*): Yes.

JEROME: I was trying terribly hard not to make love to you.

TANIS: I know.

JEROME: I'm afraid I didn't succeed very well.

TANIS (*half smiling*): I'm afraid you didn't.

JEROME: You're not angry, are you—anywhere deep down inside you? I couldn't bear that.

TANIS: No, I'm not angry.

JEROME: It would serve me right if you were.

TANIS: Why?

JEROME: I'm such an anti-romanticist—on paper.

TANIS: That doesn't count.

JEROME: If you were scared in London—I'm scared now.

TANIS (*pressing his arm lightly*): Don't be frightened, Jerry.

JEROME: We've got to behave decently—that's what's so damnable.

TANIS: Yes.

JEROME: To hell with society and all its rotten little codes.

TANIS: It isn't that either, really.

JEROME: No—I suppose it isn't.

TANIS: I'll write to you—now and again.

JEROME: Yes, please.

TANIS: Oh, don't look like that.

JEROME: Wait—I'll put up a smoke screen. (*He lights a cigarette.*)

TANIS: Good-bye, Jerry dear.

JEROME: Good-bye, Tanis dear. (*There is a pause.*) They say the new farce at the Capucines is very good.

TANIS: Yes, I heard it was.

JEROME: I went last night.

TANIS: What was it like?

JEROME: Awful!

TANIS: Yes, I heard it was. Have you seen the new Folies Bergère Revue?

JEROME: Yes, last year.

TANIS: So did I.

OWEN *enters from the street.*

OWEN: There you are, dear.

TANIS: Yes, here I am.

OWEN: Hallo, Jerry.

JEROME: You seem to have a triumphant air—as though you'd achieved something great.

OWEN: I have—I've been to Cook's.

TANIS: Thank God, at last—He's been putting it off every day.

OWEN: We leave on Thursday.

TANIS (*without enthusiasm*): Splendid!

OWEN: What do you want to go to Switzerland for, Jerry? Nasty cold place.

JEROME: The call of the snow.

OWEN: You'd much better come to Rapallo with us.

JEROME: I hate Rapallo, Owen—it's filled with double-breasted American matrons. Good-bye Tanis— we'll meet again eventually, I suppose.

TANIS: Of course we shall.

JEROME: Thank you for having lunch with me.

TANIS: I loved it.

JEROME: Good-bye, Owen.

OWEN: Good-bye. Don't climb about too much—it's bad for the liver.

JEROME: I'll remember.

> *He looks once at* TANIS *and goes off up L. quickly.*

OWEN: What do you want to do?

TANIS: I don't care.

OWEN: It's quite nice out.

TANIS: I know—I've been out.

OWEN: Well, don't snap at me—I thought we might drive round a bit.

TANIS: I must buy some stockings.

OWEN: Oh, God!

TANIS: Why not?

OWEN: You're always buying stockings.

TANIS: That's not true.

OWEN: You bought heaps the day after we arrived.

TANIS: Well, I want to buy heaps more.

OWEN: Oh, all right—come on.

TANIS: For heaven's sake, don't be so disagreeable.

OWEN: I'm not disagreeable—I merely find it a little dull standing at a crowded stocking counter surrounded by angry women.

TANIS: You can wait outside.

OWEN: Do you want to go to a play to-night?

TANIS: Yes, if you like.

OWEN (*as they go off*): We'll go to that thing at the Capucines.

CURTAIN

ACT II

SCENE II

TIME: *February. Before lunch.*

SCENE: *The Bar (same as Act I, Scene III).*

When the curtain rises the Bar is crowded. Apart from the characters already familiar to the audience there are several other groups of people smoking and talking. At a table down L. are DOROTHY *and* BERYL. CYNTHIA *and* ELISE *are sitting against the wall up R.* MARION FAWCETT, SUZANNE FELLINI *and* GEORGE HUDD *are seated together just below* ELISE *and* CYNTHIA. JEROME *is seated just above* DOROTHY *and* BERYL, *reading a paper and sipping a cocktail.* ALBERT HENNICK *is devoting himself assiduously to a rich old lady who*

is slightly deaf but determined to be vivacious. The
ensuing scene must be played simultaneously by
everybody. The dialogue being immaterial to the
play but the general effect of noise essential. INEZ
and CYRIL *are sitting silently in a corner.*

CYNTHIA:	I waited for twenty-five minutes.
ELISE:	How infuriating!
CYNTHIA:	And when she arrived with that dreadful Merrivale woman.
ELISE:	Why didn't you go?
CYNTHIA:	How could I—it would have been too pointed.
DOROTHY:	My dear, you needn't worry about that.
BERYL:	I haven't got your perfectly wonderful poise.
DOROTHY:	Nonsense!
BERYL:	It's true—I get embarrassed terribly easily.
DOROTHY:	I wish you'd telephoned me.
ALBERT:	It's really worth seeing.
OLD LADY:	What?
ALBERT:	I say it's really worth seeing— she's entrancing.
OLD LADY:	I didn't know it was a musical play.
ALBERT:	It isn't.
OLD LADY:	You said she was dancing——
MARION:	Never again as long as I live.
GEORGE:	It was damn funny though.
MARION:	It may have been to you—I was furious.

SUZANNE: { She always gets bad-tempered when she's drunk.

GEORGE: I couldn't help laughing——

ELISE: I can't understand what she sees in her.

CYNTHIA: Neither can anyone else.

ELISE: It's that sort of mind that prevents her being a good artiste.

CYNTHIA: She's never real for a moment.

ELISE: She deceives a lot of people though—Freddie Carrol was raving about her——

BERYL: I will another time.

DOROTHY: You see I've known him for years.

BERYL: Yes, he said heavenly things about you.

DOROTHY: That's damn nice of him.

BERYL: But he did—honestly.

ALBERT: No—entrancing—marvellous.

OLD LADY: I love anything a little risqué.

ALBERT: Well, it's certainly that.

OLD LADY: What?

ALBERT: I say it's certainly that.

OLD LADY: What a pity—she used to be so lovely.

SUZANNE: I must say I see Marion's point.

GEORGE: Who was the little fair girl who sang?

MARION: I don't know—she made me feel uncomfortable.

SUZANNE: Marie something or other—she used to be at the Casino de Paris.

GEORGE: Damned attractive-looking!

ALBERT: Shall we go and have lunch now?
OLD LADY: What?
ALBERT: Lunch?
OLD LADY: Oh yes—I'm dieting, you know—
                        I shan't eat much.
ALBERT (*rising*):   I'm not particularly hungry.
OLD LADY: We might walk through to the
                        Restaurant.

    ALBERT *pilots her out.*

SUZANNE: Thanks for the cocktail, George—
                        I wish you were eating with us.
GEORGE: I shall wait ten minutes more.
MARION (*rising*):   Come on, Suzanne.
SUZANNE: Give us a call when you get back.
GEORGE: We'll have a party.

MARION: Lovely. Good-bye.

GEORGE: I shall probably be at the Crillon—I'm sick of this place.

SUZANNE: So am I—but it's a sort of habit one can't shake off.

    SUZANNE *and* MARION *go out—leaving* GEORGE *at the table. Several other people have left by this time, so the atmosphere has become less congested and the individual dialogue easier to distinguish.* GEORGE *catches* BERYL'S *eye—she nods to him and smiles.* DOROTHY *looks over and waves.*

BERYL: He's nice, isn't he?

DOROTHY: Who—George?

BERYL: Yes.

DOROTHY: Not bad.

BERYL: He was sweet to me at that party.

DOROTHY: I think you made a hit.

BERYL: Do you—really?

DOROTHY: Not that you had much chance with Harry hanging round you all the time.

BERYL: Harry's getting on my nerves—he's so possessive.

DOROTHY: Never mind, dear.

BERYL: I should never have rowed with Marion if it hadn't been for him.

DOROTHY: I didn't know you had.

BERYL: We're not speaking now—Didn't you see her sweep out just then without looking at me?

DOROTHY: She's no loss to anyone—are you doing anything to-night—late?

BERYL: I'm supposed to be supping with Harry—why?

DOROTHY: I wondered if you'd do me a great favour.

BERYL: Of course. What is it?

DOROTHY: Come out with Julius and me—I daren't be seen with him alone when Mike's in Paris.

BERYL: I'll have to put off Harry.

DOROTHY: Does it matter?

BERYL: Not much—I'll telephone him.

DOROTHY: You're a dear.

BERYL: You've been perfectly darling to me.

DOROTHY: I like you.

GEORGE *rises and comes over to their table.*

GEORGE: Hallo, Dorothy.

DOROTHY: Oh, hallo.

GEORGE: Good morning, Miss Fletcher—may I join you for a moment?

DOROTHY: Of course.

He sits down.

GEORGE: Will you both have a cocktail with me?

BERYL: No, thank you.

DOROTHY: I've already had two—I'm waiting for Mike.

GEORGE (*to* BERYL): Are you lunching anywhere?

BERYL: Yes—I'm afraid I am.

GEORGE: I'm sorry—I thought you might have lunched with me.

BERYL: It's terribly sweet of you—I should have loved to—but . . .

GEORGE: I'm leaving Paris on Friday.

BERYL (*disappointed*): Oh—what a shame.

DOROTHY: What time did you say you'd meet Harry?

BERYL: One o'clock.

DOROTHY (*glancing at her watch*): It's nearly half-past.

BERYL: Harry's always late.

GEORGE: Rotten bad manners.

BERYL: Yes, I suppose it is.

DOROTHY: I'm sorry you're leaving so soon, George.

GEORGE (*looking at* BERYL): So am I—damned sorry.

DOROTHY: Listen—I've got an appointment at two o'clock anyhow. Why don't we three lunch together—it'll teach Mike and Harry a lesson.

BERYL: Oh, Dorothy!

GEORGE: I wish you would.

DOROTHY: Come on—we'll go somewhere quiet.

BERYL: I ought to wait really.

DOROTHY: Don't be a fool, dear—do what you want to do.

BERYL: He'll be furious.

DOROTHY: So will Mike—serve them right.

GEORGE: I've got to buy a birthday present for my sister this afternoon—you might help me to choose it.

BERYL: Can't I leave a message or anything?

DOROTHY: Tell the doorman to say you couldn't wait any longer.

BERYL: All right—let's go quickly.

They go out.

GEORGE *squeezes* DOROTHY'S *arm gratefully.*

TANIS *comes in as they go out. She goes over to* JEROME.

JEROME (*rising*): My dear.

TANIS: Well, Jerry?

JEROME: I wondered if you'd come.

TANIS: That was silly of you.

JEROME: You have a tremendously stern conscience at moments. I felt a bit apprehensive.

TANIS: I think my conscience must have died.

JEROME: When?

TANIS: You know when.

JEROME: You're exultant and defiant to-day—I do love you for it.

TANIS: I'm extraordinarily happy—you see, it hasn't been entirely our fault—we put up a good fight at first. There was no reason for me ever to have known you were here if Fate hadn't led us both to the opera on Monday.

JEROME: It's cowardly to blame Fate—and yet I'm inclined to agree with you.

TANIS: Dear Jerry.

JEROME: Don't use that voice to me when there are other people about—it isn't fair.

TANIS: I told Owen I was lunching with you.

JEROME: Did you?

TANIS: Yes, here.

JEROME: If he tries to find us—he'll search in vain.

TANIS: I'm afraid he will.

They go out.

MIKE *enters hurriedly—looks round and sits at table down L.* ELISE *and* CYNTHIA *rise and walk out.*

ELISE (*as they go*): What's the use of arguing?

CYNTHIA: No use at all—obviously.

ELISE: Why do it then?

CYNTHIA: You're impossible.

ELISE: I'm honest—anyhow.

CYNTHIA: I wonder!

They go out.

MIKE (*calling* WAITER): Garçon!

WAITER: Monsieur?

MIKE: You know Miss Price, don't you?

WAITER: Yes, monsieur.

MIKE: Has she been here this morning?

WAITER (*thinking*): Yes, monsieur—she went out a few minutes ago.

MIKE: Was she alone.

WAITER: No, monsieur—there was a lady and gentleman.

MIKE: A dark gentleman?

WAITER: I don't remember, monsieur.

MIKE: She left no message.

WAITER: Non, monsieur.

MIKE: All right.

The WAITER *departs.*

MIKE *rises angrily and is about to go out when* HARRY *enters.*

HARRY: Hallo!

MIKE: Hallo!

HARRY: What's the matter?

MIKE: Nothing.

HARRY: Come and have a drink.

MIKE: No, thanks.

He goes out and leaves HARRY *looking after him in some surprise.* HARRY *looks round Bar for* BERYL, *then with an exclamation of annoyance, goes out.*

INEZ *and* CYRIL *rise and go towards the door back.*

INEZ: I believe that in some people a sullen silence is considered rather attractive. Cyril darling, in your case I find it a little irritating.

CYRIL (*impatiently*): Oh, I'm sorry.

INEZ: So am I—and very hurt.

CYRIL: Now look here, Inez.

INEZ: I'm beginning to realise that you've cheated with me.

As they reach the door, NORMA *enters hurriedly.*

CYRIL (*his voice changing*): Norma!

NORMA (*glancing at him and then at* INEZ): Oh, hallo——(*She walks down and seats herself at a table.*)

CYRIL *hesitates, looking at her.*

INEZ (*at door*): Cyril——

CYRIL (*hopelessly*): All right—I'm coming.

They go out.

NORMA *pulls off her gloves and summons a* WAITER.

NORMA: Garçon.

WAITER: Madame?

NORMA: Bring me a Bronx, please.

WAITER: One, madame?

NORMA (*as an afterthought*): You'd better bring two.

WAITER: Bien, madame.

He whips up two used glasses from her table and departs. NORMA *lights a cigarette and waits.* OWEN *enters.*

61

NORMA: Beautifully timed.

OWEN: Have you only just arrived?

NORMA: A minute ago—I ordered you a Bronx.

OWEN: Splendid!

NORMA: I'm dead—I've been rushing about all the morning.

OWEN: So am I—we'll both relax completely.

NORMA: Thank God, there's no one here—I get so sick of people all over the place.

OWEN: It's a tiring spot Paris—do you mind if I have one of your cigarettes?—I've run out.

NORMA: Of course not—here.

She pushes her case along the table to him—he looks at her and smiles.

CURTAIN

ACT II

SCENE III

TIME: *June.*

SCENE: *The scene is a corner of the terrace outside the Grill Room. There are only three tables visible—the one down R. is in the sun and is protected by a large umbrella. The one down L. is occupied by* SUZANNE FELLINI *and* DOROTHY. *The one above it is empty, as is also the one down R.*

DOROTHY: I don't know what to do.

SUZANNE: Well, I gave you advice before and you were furious with me.

DOROTHY: That was different.

SUZANNE: No, it wasn't.

DOROTHY: What shall I do now? I think I'm going crazy.

SUZANNE: Leave Paris.

DOROTHY: You know I can't.

SUZANNE: Why not?

DOROTHY: I should never see him again.

SUZANNE: Exactly.

DOROTHY: It's all very fine for you to sit there and say "exactly". You don't know how I feel.

SUZANNE: Yes, I do—but you must pull yourself together.

DOROTHY (*almost crying*): I can't—I can't.

SUZANNE: Listen, dear—you're no fool—you know perfectly well he's using you.

DOROTHY: I don't care—I love him.

SUZANNE: Mike's as crazy about you as ever he was— why can't you be satisfied with that?

DOROTHY: Mike drives me mad.

SUZANNE: Only because you give way to it—if Julius weren't about, you'd be all right.

DOROTHY: Oh, Suzanne—I'm so damned miserable——

SUZANNE: You wouldn't be for long if you made a real effort and got away.

DOROTHY: You think Julius doesn't love me a bit.

SUZANNE: That's not the point.

DOROTHY: It *is* the point—do you think that?

SUZANNE: I don't know him well enough to judge—

but I do know that if you let Mike go on his account, you're mad.

DOROTHY: Mike need never know.

SUZANNE: He suspects now.

DOROTHY: How do you know?

SUZANNE: Of course he does—and there'll be trouble soon, bad trouble.

DOROTHY: I'm not afraid of him.

SUZANNE: I am.

DOROTHY: What could he do anyhow?

SUZANNE: That depends how drunk he is when he finds out.

DOROTHY: Here comes that little fool Beryl Fletcher with George.

SUZANNE: I must go—Come round to the flat at tea time.

DOROTHY: All right.

SUZANNE: And for God's sake think over what I've said.

> GEORGE *and* BERYL *come up to the table.* BERYL *is wearing pearls and some expensive bangles.*

BERYL: We had to come over and say hallo.

SUZANNE (*shaking hands with* GEORGE): How are you, George?

GEORGE: Fine! We're going down to Le Touquet this afternoon.

BERYL: George gambles terribly.

GEORGE: Pretty successfully though, just lately. How's everything, Dorothy?

DOROTHY: Rotten, thanks.

SUZANNE: Dorothy's got a hangover today.

DOROTHY (*with some malice*): I saw Harry yesterday.

BERYL (*sweetly*): Did you? How was he?

DOROTHY: He seemed very bright.

BERYL: Poor old Harry.

DOROTHY: Come on Suzanne—we must be going.

BERYL (*as they all four go out*): We're going to be in Deauville all July. George has taken the cutest little villa you've ever seen—you must come and stay—mustn't they, George?

GEORGE: Oh yes, rather.

> *They go off.*
>
> *During the latter part of their scene* OWEN *and* NORMA *have entered and sat at the table down R.* OWEN *is ordering lunch—with the* MAÎTRE D'HÔ- TEL.

OWEN: Two canteloup . . .

MAÎTRE (*writing it down*): Bien, monsieur.

OWEN: What then, Norma?

NORMA: Something frightfully light and cool. I'm not a bit hungry.

OWEN: Cold soup?

NORMA: No—no soup—just one thing and a salad.

MAÎTRE: A little cold duckling.

NORMA: Yes, that'll do.

OWEN: Very well—duckling for two.

NORMA: And ordinary cœur de laitue with French dressing.

MAÎTRE: Entremets?

OWEN: We'll decide afterwards.

MAÎTRE: Very well, monsieur.

> *He goes away.*

OWEN: I do loathe ordering things.

NORMA: So do I.

OWEN: I feel awfully gay this morning.

NORMA: Do you, Owen?

OWEN: Yes. I've been arguing for days with fat German business men and now out of a clear sky, I find myself lunching with you.

NORMA (*smiling*): How lovely for you.

OWEN: It is—really.

NORMA: You're a strange man.

OWEN: Why strange?

NORMA: I didn't like you much at first.

OWEN: Do you now?

NORMA: Of course—you were awfully sweet when we were all here in February.

OWEN: Friendships take a long time to build up—I was frightened of you.

NORMA: Frightened?

OWEN: Yes—you seemed so sure and determined—I watched that poor young Cyril Hardacre battering his head against your supreme detachment.

NORMA: That sounds frightfully attractive, I'm afraid he didn't batter much, though.

OWEN: You were rather unkind to him, weren't you?

NORMA: No.

OWEN: A little heartless?

NORMA: I don't believe in pretending things I don't feel.

OWEN: There comes a time when one has to.

A WAITER arrives with the melon.

NORMA: It does look delicious, doesn't it?

OWEN: Beautiful.

NORMA: Cyril's terribly weak anyhow—I hate weak people.

OWEN: You make me feel fearfully old at moments.

NORMA: Sorry.

OWEN: When do you leave for Biarritz?

NORMA: To-morrow—then Father and I are coming back through Spain.

OWEN: Is he working on a new book there?

NORMA: Supposed to be—but he's awfully lazy. How's Tanis?

OWEN: All right—I had a card from her two days ago in Berlin.

NORMA: Is she in London?

OWEN: Yes.

NORMA: Give her my love.

OWEN: Of course I will.

NORMA: I don't think she likes me much.

OWEN: Nonsense—why shouldn't she?

NORMA: I have a feeling about it.

OWEN: I'm sure you're wrong.

NORMA: I wish I knew you better—there are so many things I should like to say to you.

OWEN: You can say anything you want to.

NORMA: No, I can't—not yet.

OWEN: Why not?

NORMA: We've met so often casually in crowds—I feel tongue-tied when we're alone.

OWEN: You needn't a bit.

NORMA: I'm so desperately curious about you.

OWEN: Curious?

NORMA: Yes, it's cheap of me, I know—but I'm longing to know about you really—private, personal things.

OWEN: What, for instance?

NORMA: Well—are you in love with Tanis?

OWEN: Norma!

NORMA: I'm sorry—I was afraid you'd be embarrassed.

OWEN: I'm not embarrassed—only rather surprised.

NORMA: You're quite right—I deserve to be snubbed—please forgive me and let's talk about something else.

OWEN: Why did you ask that?

NORMA: Sheer cheap curiosity.

OWEN: Of course I'm in love with Tanis.

NORMA: That's all right then, isn't it?

OWEN: How do you mean?

NORMA: Here comes the duckling.

The WAITER *serves duckling and salad and takes away remains of melon.*

OWEN: Is your salad all right?

NORMA: Grand, thanks.

OWEN: I thought you were probably going to marry Cyril.

NORMA: You were wrong.

OWEN: He's a nice boy.

NORMA: Yes—but I don't love him.

OWEN: That might come afterwards.

NORMA: I doubt it.

OWEN: Why?

NORMA: Things don't pan out as easily as that.

OWEN: He's got a nice private income, hasn't he?

NORMA: Don't be horrid.

OWEN: Are you in love with someone else?

NORMA: Yes.

OWEN: Oh, I see.

NORMA: No, you don't.

OWEN: I'm being curious now.

NORMA: I know.

OWEN: Fairly itching with it.

68

NORMA: Owen, we'd really better talk about something quite different.

OWEN: It's more interesting talking about ourselves.

NORMA: You headed me off just now when I wanted to.

OWEN: No, I didn't.

NORMA: Yes, you did—you told me a smart little lie.

OWEN: You mean about Tanis?

NORMA: Yes.

OWEN: What does it matter anyway?

NORMA: A good deal.

OWEN: I'm sorry.

NORMA: Has the drifting apart been mutual?

OWEN: Yes, I think so.

NORMA: Poor Owen.

OWEN: You're behaving awfully badly, Norma.

NORMA: Yes, I suppose I am.

OWEN: Why are you?

NORMA: Don't you know?

OWEN: I half guess—but I'm not sure.

NORMA: I love you.

OWEN (*smiling at her*): My dear—how ridiculous of you.

NORMA: I expect it is—but it can't be helped.

OWEN: I don't know what to do now.

NORMA: It is rather awkward, isn't it?

OWEN: Damnably.

NORMA: I suppose the whole lunch is going to be a failure now owing to my lack of restraint.

OWEN: We'll try not to let it be.

NORMA: I had to tell you, you know—it's been going on inside me for months.

OWEN: That's an awfully nice hat.

NORMA: I'm glad you like it—I bought it yesterday morning.

OWEN (*suddenly resting his hand on hers*): Do you want anything more to eat—darling?

NORMA (*emotionally*): Owen! (*She buries her head in her arms.*)

OWEN: Don't, dear—don't be silly——

CURTAIN

ACT III

Scene I

TIME: *January 1926.*

SCENE: *The scene is the Men's Bar—Rue Gilon side. It is before dinner. On the left of the stage is a bar with two men in white coats serving drinks. The entrance is on the right. There are tables along the back wall.*

When the curtain rises, HARRY LEFTWICH *and* GEORGE HUDD *are drinking at the bar down left. At a table up right are a fair young man and a dark young man, engrossed in conversation.* JULIUS LEVENOVITCH *finishes a drink, glances at his wrist watch and goes out.* GEORGE *and* HARRY *turn to look after him.*

GEORGE: What women can see in that beats me.

HARRY: He's just one of those mournful Russians—they're always successful.

GEORGE: Shifty-looking swine.

HARRY: Is Dorothy Price still playing around with him?

GEORGE: Yes, I think so.

HARRY: He's probably getting a good bit out of her.

GEORGE: Well, good luck to him if she's such a fool.

HARRY: Have another?

GEORGE: All right.

HARRY: Two more Martinis with a dash.

GEORGE: No dash for me.

BARMAN: Very good, sir.

  BEVERLEY *and* ALBERT *enter and cross to the bar.*

ALBERT: And we'd just got half way down the street when I realised what the game was.

BEVERLEY: My God!

ALBERT: I was terrified.

BEVERLEY: What did you do?

ALBERT: I turned and ran, my dear.

BEVERLEY: You should have been more careful.

ALBERT: Well, how was I to know? It was all Eric's fault anyhow.

BEVERLEY: What do you want?

ALBERT: A Manhattan, please. I love the little cherry at the bottom.

BEVERLEY: One Manhattan, one Bronx.

BARMAN: Very good, sir.

BEVERLEY: Jimmy's got a party to-night.

ALBERT: I *know* he'll be turned out of that flat.

  CYRIL *enters and crosses to bar.*

BEVERLEY: Hallo, Cyril—want a cocktail?

CYRIL: Yes, thanks.

BEVERLEY: Manhattan?

CYRIL: Yes, that'll do.

BEVERLEY: Another Manhattan.

BARMAN: Yes, sir.

  The other BARMAN *serves drinks to* GEORGE *and* HARRY.

HARRY: Here you are.

GEORGE: Thanks.

HARRY: Here's how.

GEORGE: Cheerio.

ALBERT: How's Inez, Cyril?

CYRIL: I don't know—I haven't seen her for ages.

BEVERLEY: Your little friend Norma What's-her-name is in Paris.

CYRIL (*looking up sharply*): Is she?

ALBERT: Startled fawn very difficult.

BEVERLEY: Don't tease Cyril, Albert—we must all try to be broadminded.

CYRIL: Is she staying here?

BEVERLEY: How do I know?

CYRIL: You generally know everything about everybody.

BEVERLEY: Only the people I'm interested in.

> *The* BARMAN *brings them their cocktails—*BEVERLEY *pays for them.*

> GEORGE *and* HARRY *stroll out.*

> LUKE BELLOWS *enters with* JOSHUA DRAKE. LUKE *is a good-looking young man of about twenty-eight; his clothes are sack-like. He possesses a rugged, boyish charm enhanced by a Middle Western accent.* JOSHUA DRAKE *is small and fair and untidy.*

ALBERT: Why, Luke! This is marvellous!

LUKE: Hallo, Albert.

ALBERT: When did you arrive?

LUKE: Yesterday on the *Leviathan.*

JOSHUA: I found him wandering along the Rue Castiligone.

ALBERT: Do you know Beverley Ford—Luke Bellows.

LUKE: Glad to meet you, Mr. Ford.

> *They shake hands.*

BEVERLEY: I've heard of you, of course—hundreds of times.

LUKE: That's terribly nice of you.

ALBERT: When are you playing again?

LUKE: Not until the Fall—I'm going over to London. They want me to do *Chummy* there.

ALBERT: They'd love you. He's marvellous in *Chummy*, Beverley.

LUKE: Do you think they would like me—honestly?

ALBERT: Of course.

LUKE: I guess I'm not elegant enough for London.

JOSHUA: Don't take any notice of him—he always goes on like that—it's a stunt.

LUKE (*winsomely*): Isn't Paris wonderful?

JOSHUA: Let's all go and sit down, for God's sake.

They all go over to table up left and order drinks.

Enter BENNY TYRELL *and* FREDDY PALMER.

BENNY is about thirty; FREDDY *about twenty-two. They cross straight over to the bar.*

BENNY: What d'you want?

FREDDY: Champagne cocktail.

BENNY: Two champagne cocktails.

BARMAN: Yes, sir.

BENNY (*looking across at* LUKE): Now I know why you wanted to come here.

FREDDY: Don't start a scene.

BENNY: I suppose you're going to pretend.

FREDDY: I'm not pretending anything.

LUKE (*rising*): Excuse me a moment. (*He comes over.*) Hallo, Freddy.

FREDDY: Hallo.

LUKE: How do you feel after the boat, Benny?

BENNY: Splendid, thanks—You look much better.

LUKE: Why don't you both come and lunch with me to-morrow—I'm just a boy from the West alone in Paris.

74

BENNY: I can't.

LUKE: What about you, Freddy?

FREDDY: All right.

BENNY: I can't wait any longer for the cocktails; I must go.

> *He goes.*

LUKE: Sorry if I was butting in.

FREDDY: Benny's in a bad temper to-day, anyhow.

LUKE: Did you get the photographs?

FREDDY: Yes.

LUKE: Did you like them?

FREDDY: Here are the cocktails—you'd better take Benny's.

LUKE: Thanks—I wish you weren't so tied up.

FREDDY: I'm not really, but——

LUKE: You're so determined not to be friends.

FREDDY: I explained on the boat.

LUKE: Well, I can wait, Freddy old kid. (*He raises glass.*) Les Printemps.

FREDDY: Le Printemps.

LUKE: All right—I know your French is better than mine.

ALBERT (*calling*): Luke—do come and sit down.

LUKE: Come over and join us.

FREDDY: No, thanks—I must go and find Benny.

> LUKE *rejoins his friends.* FREDDY *pays for the cocktails and departs.*
>
> OWEN *and* JEROME *enter and cross over to the bar.*

OWEN: You're right about this place—I'm sick to death of it.

JEROME: We're far more comfortable at the Crillon than we ever were here.

OWEN: I know—Norma told me.

JEROME: What shall we drink?

OWEN: Something innocuous.

JEROME: Martinis are safe and conventional.

OWEN: All right.

JEROME: Two Martinis.

BARMAN: Yes, sir.

JEROME: Why are you so depressed?

OWEN: Am I?

JEROME: Yes, I think so.

OWEN: I find life rather too hectic.

JEROME: You've never struck me as being a particularly hectic type.

OWEN: That's the trouble—I'm not.

JEROME: People like me who write and are supposed to have temperament always resent nerves in anyone else.

OWEN: I'm sorry, Jerry.

JEROME: Don't apologise.

OWEN: As a matter of fact, Paris doesn't seem to be stimulating you quite as much as usual this time.

JEROME: I'm beginning to hate it—I'm only waiting for something definite to happen.

OWEN: What sort of something?

JEROME: Some crisis—then I shall go away—thousands of miles—no more soft carpets and shaded lights and civilised conversation——

OWEN: The great open spaces?

JEROME: Yes, where men are men.

OWEN (laughing): You mustn't let this bar dishearten you.

JEROME: Oh, these don't matter—they're not even

real of their kind—here's your drink. (*He pays the* BARMAN.)

BARMAN: Thank you, sir.

JEROME: I find it so difficult not to cheat when everyone else is cheating all round me.

OWEN: How do you mean?

JEROME: I expect you'll know some day.

OWEN: I'm more used to you when you're intellectually superior and sure of yourself.

JEROME: I suppose I am letting down a bit.

OWEN: Anyhow I don't know you at all, really.

JEROME: Neither do I.

OWEN: Strange bird.

JEROME: Thanks.

OWEN: Did you take that as a compliment?

JEROME: No—merely as a contribution to the conversation. I was duly grateful.

OWEN: You've always found me dull, haven't you?

JEROME: Not dull exactly—rather difficult.

OWEN: That's putting it nicely.

JEROME: All right, dull then.

OWEN: You've irritated me a good deal from time to time.

JEROME (*smiling*): I expect I have.

OWEN: I suppose I was envious of your knowledge of things and people.

JEROME: You needn't have been—that sort of knowledge only complicates one's own problems doubly.

OWEN: Cheer up!

   JULIUS *re-enters hurriedly and crosses to bar; he looks very white and rather scared.*

JULIUS: Give me a brandy and soda, please.

BARMAN: Yes, sir.

JULIUS: Double.

BARMAN: Right, sir.

JEROME: I suppose we'd better go. Tanis will be waiting.

OWEN: I doubt it—but we'll see.

There is a scream of laughter from LUKE *and* JOSHUA *and* ALBERT *at something* BEVERLEY *has said.*

BEVERLEY: I always said it was worse than madness to shave off his moustache.

ALBERT: Jimmy wouldn't speak to him for days.

There is more laughter. JEROME *and* OWEN *have just reached the door when* MIKE CRAVEN *bursts in, followed by* GEORGE HUDD. MIKE *is obviously drunk; he bangs into* JEROME *without apologising.*

JEROME (*glancing at him*): Don't mention it.

He and OWEN *go out.*

MIKE: Where is he?

GEORGE (*endeavouring to calm him*): Don't be a fool, Mike.

MIKE *goes up to* JULIUS *and swings him round.*

MIKE: Here, you!

GEORGE: Mike—for God's sake.

JULIUS: Take your hands off me.

MIKE: Come outside then, you swine!

JULIUS (*trying to push past him*): Leave me alone.

MIKE: I'll knock your damned head off.

GEORGE: Shut up, Mike.

JULIUS: You're drunk!

MIKE *takes up* JULIUS' *drink and flings it in his face.* BEVERLEY, JOSHUA *and* ALBERT *and* LUKE *rise hurriedly.*

MIKE: I'll teach you to muck about with my women!

78

ALBERT: My God, there's a row on.

LUKE: Let's get out—I don't want to be mixed up in anything.

JULIUS (*white with rage and terror*): You'll regret that.

MIKE: Pimp! Crawling bloody pimp!

    He takes a revolver from his pocket and shoots JULIUS. *There is a scream from* ALBERT *and a concerted rush for the door.* JULIUS *falls down. A* BARMAN *vaults over the bar and assisted by* GEORGE *wrenches the revolver from* MIKE's *hand. The other* BARMAN *rushes out. The dark young man and the fair young man disappear behind their table.*

MIKE (*beside himself*): I'll show him—I'll show him——

GEORGE (*kneeling beside* JULIUS): Fetch a doctor, quick!

QUICK CURTAIN

ACT III

SCENE II

TIME: *The same night. It is about 3 a.m.*

SCENE: *The Lounge, Rue Gilon side, same as Act II, Scene I.*

    *The stage is empty—*INEZ *and* VIOLET EMERY *enter from the communicating passage up left. They are both in evening dress.* VIOLET *is extremely chic and*

79

wearing excellent jewellery.

VIOLET: It was divine of you to drop me.

INEZ: We ought to have told the taxi to come to this entrance really.

VIOLET: I know—I never thought of it.

INEZ: It's been charming—meeting you. I've heard so much about you from Mary.

VIOLET: Not too much, I hope; so many things are spoiled by people saying too much.

INEZ: Will you lunch or dine with me sometime?

VIOLET: I should love to.

INEZ: Very well—I'll telephone you.

VIOLET: Any time before eleven thirty.

INEZ: Well, good-bye.

VIOLET: I suppose you wouldn't come up and talk to me while I go to bed—I'm wide awake.

INEZ: The taxi's waiting.

VIOLET: You could ring down from my room and have him sent away—the night porter will pay him.

INEZ: Just for a few minutes, then.

VIOLET (*ringing for the lift*): You're an awfully sympathetic person.

INEZ (*smiling*): Am I?

VIOLET: I felt it the moment you came into the room to-night.

INEZ: With all those people chattering?

VIOLET: That didn't matter.

INEZ: I'm glad.

VIOLET: And of course when you sang...

INEZ: Here's the lift.

> *They enter the lift and disappear.*
> SUZANNE FELLINI *enters from right. She is in*

*travelling clothes. She glances at her watch, then sits
on the sofa. A group of people pass through talking
and go off up left.* DOROTHY *comes out of the lift,
also in travelling clothes. She carries a small jewel
case.*

DOROTHY: I saw you arrive—I've been at the window
for hours.

SUZANNE: Are there any more developments?

DOROTHY: No, I haven't heard a thing—the telephone rang several times but I didn't answer it.

SUZANNE: Has the manager been up to see you?

DOROTHY: No—I don't think my name can have
been mentioned yet.

SUZANNE: You can come to my flat until the train
goes.

DOROTHY: You've been wonderful to me, Suzanne—
I'll never forget it.

SUZANNE: Lucky for you he didn't kill him.

    They go off hurriedly right.

    JEROME *and* TANIS *enter. They are in evening
    dress.*

TANIS: Good-night, my dear—you were a darling to
bring me back.

JEROME (*holding her hand*): Don't be silly.

TANIS: By the way, where have we been?

JEROME: Oh, anywhere.

TANIS: Zelli's?

JEROME: It was Zelli's last time.

TANIS: Let's invent somewhere; we can always forget
how to find it if anyone wants us to take them.

JEROME: La Grotte Bleu?

TANIS: Too obvious.

JEROME: Le Parapluie Vert?

TANIS: Lovely—the colour helps.

JEROME: Gypsies sang to us.

TANIS: Of course they did—Darling, I do love you.

JEROME: Shhh!

TANIS: Telephone me in the morning.

She goes towards the lift and meets OWEN *and* NORMA *coming out of it.* OWEN *gives a start of embarrassment.*

Owen—I thought you were in bed?

OWEN: I felt better so I got up again—you're very late.

NORMA (*with great sang froid*): Hallo, Father.

JEROME: Where have you been?

NORMA: Talking to Owen.

JEROME: How long have you been talking to him?

NORMA (*casually*): I don't know—I went home to the Crillon after I left Ethel's party and you weren't there, so I called up Owen.

TANIS: What an odd thing to do.

JEROME: When did you come to the Crillon?

NORMA: About half an hour ago.

JEROME (*quickly*): Is this true, Owen?

NORMA: Father! What on earth's the matter?

OWEN: Of course it's true.

JEROME: How long has Norma been with you?

NORMA (*faintly flurried*): Father, don't be so absurd.

OWEN: Only a little while—she just told you.

NORMA: I told you I went back to the hotel and you weren't there, and I wasn't a bit sleepy so . . .

JEROME: That's a lie—I was there.

TANIS: Jerry!

JEROME: I've been there for the last two hours.

OWEN: Where were you then, Tanis?

82

TANIS: This is all perfectly ridiculous—I'm going to bed.

OWEN: Where you at the Crillon, too?

TANIS: Certainly not. I . . .

JEROME: We'd all better stop lying now—Tanis was at the Crillon with me.

OWEN: Tanis!

TANIS: Don't look like that, Owen—you don't mind really.

OWEN (aghast): You mean——?

JEROME (quickly): I am your wife's lover, Owen.

OWEN: My God!

JEROME: That remark has no longer any dramatic significance—one says it when one can't find a taxi.

OWEN: Tanis, please go up to our room.

JEROME: You're so unconscious of irony—it's pathetic.

OWEN: Shut up, you cad!

JEROME: We've been lovers for months—oblivious to everything but one another—that's why we're all here in this vile situation. When did you seduce Norma, Owen?—Was it to-night or ages ago?—Let's be frank and outspoken . . .

NORMA (clutching his arm): Father!

JEROME (pushing her aside): Keep away from me—we must all be calm and just and honest with one another. I feel terribly wise and ashamed just for a moment—it won't last—nothing lasts ever—I shall creep back to the usual refuge of codes and pretences—utter futility. It's quite natural really. We're all silly animals, gratifying our own beastly desires, covering them with a veneer of decency and good behaviour. Lies—lies—complete rottenness . . .

TANIS: For God's sake, stop talking like that!

JEROME (*laughing*): Why—it's true, isn't it?—I'm your lover—Owen is Norma's lover. Owen's your husband—Norma's my daughter—there's real life for you—love—romance—beauty—happy ever after ...

OWEN: How dare you talk like that—you've no proof.

JEROME: I don't need proof—I have a splendid knack of knowing things by instinct—it earns me my daily bread.

OWEN (*stubbornly*): It's not true—I don't love Norma.

JEROME: If you lie any more, I shall strangle you.

NORMA: Stop, Owen—don't say a word.

TANIS (*sinking into the sofa, burying her face in her hands*): Horrible—horrible—horrible——

JEROME: There's nothing to be done, you know—nothing at all. We might of course start our lives all over again—that would be interesting—or we might rush into convents and monasteries and repent in religious seclusion—hasn't anyone a suggestion to make—I don't wish to monopolise the conversation.

NORMA (*crying*): Stop, Father—please, please, stop——

OWEN: Come away, Tanis.

JEROME: That's right—take her away—please, please, take her away.

> OWEN *and* TANIS *go towards the lift.* NORMA *stands still, sobbing.* MR. *and* MRS. JEVON *enter from right; they are a young married couple.*

MRS. JEVON (*recognising* JEROME): Why, Mr. Kennedy—I'd no idea you were in Paris.

JEROME: We're leaving to-morrow.

MRS. JEVON: Well, isn't that a pity now. I should have loved to see something of you. This is my husband—I don't think you've met.

MR. JEVON: How do you do.

They shake hands.

MRS. JEVON: Paris is terrible—one never gets any sleep.

MR. JEVON: The lift's just going up.

MRS. JEVON: All right—good-night, Mr. Kennedy— perhaps we shall see something of you in London?

JEROME: Delightful! Good-night.

MR. JEVON: Good-night.

JEROME: Good-night.

They go to the lift and disappear with TANIS *and* OWEN.

NORMA *has been standing by the window with her back turned; she turns.* JEROME *clasps her in his arms.*

NORMA: Father!

JEROME: Oh, Christ!

CURTAIN

ACT III

SCENE III

TIME: *June. It is late afternoon.*

SCENE: *The Lounge (Place du Cœur side). The same as Act I, Scene I.*

NORMA *is writing at the bureau. A* YOUNG MAN *is seated down right, reading an illustrated paper. He occasionally glances up as though expecting someone. Music can be heard from the direction of the Tea Lounge. A group of people come in through the swing doors. Finally a* YOUNG GIRL *comes in. The* YOUNG MAN *rises.*

YOUNG MAN: I thought you were never coming.

YOUNG GIRL: I couldn't get away—Mother's gone home to rest.

YOUNG MAN: It's awfully late.

YOUNG GIRL: Don't be angry.

YOUNG MAN: I'm not, but . . .

YOUNG GIRL: You are—just a little.

YOUNG MAN: Come along.

YOUNG GIRL: I ought to telephone really—I'm supposed to be having tea with Mrs. Banks.

YOUNG MAN: Not now—please not now.

YOUNG GIRL: All right.

They go out through the swing doors.

LUKE BELLOWS *and* FREDDY PALMER *enter. The* DAY PORTER *brings their bags after them.*

LUKE: Have you got any change?

FREDDY: Yes.

LUKE: Tip him then, will you?

FREDDY: All right. (*He does so.*)

LUKE: Leave them here till we find the number of our room, then we'll send a bell boy.

PORTER: Yes, sir. Thank you, sir.

LUKE: Isn't Paris marvellous—one gets a thrill every time.

FREDDY: Yes.

LUKE: Are you happy?

FREDDY: Of course.

ALBERT HENNICK *appears from direction of Lounge.*

ALBERT (*effusively*): Luke—my dear, this is divine. I thought it was you but I wasn't sure—Hallo, Freddy.

FREDDY: Hallo.

LUKE (*obviously*): We just arrived a minute ago.

ALBERT: That's grand—Jimmy's giving a party to-night—you must both come.

FREDDY: Jimmy who?

ALBERT: Jimmy Collett—you don't mean to say you don't know Jimmy?

LUKE: We've neither of us been here since January.

ALBERT: Of course you haven't. Jimmy came in March from Rome—he was going to be a priest and now he isn't—you'll adore him.

LUKE: We're only staying a few days.

ALBERT: He's living with Bob Trevor—you know Bob, don't you?

FREDDY: Yes, I do.

LUKE: I don't...

ALBERT: He's a scream—like a great Newfoundland puppy, melting eyes and a divine sense of humour—Is it true you're going to play *Ghosts* in New York with Myra Pelly?

LUKE: Yes, I think so—we're going to give alternate performances.

FREDDY: I can't see Myra Pelly as a boy.

ALBERT: Never mind. I'm sure *she* can.

LUKE: Come and help us find out about our room.

ALBERT (*as they go up back*): How's Benny?

FREDDY (*stiffly*): I don't know; I haven't seen him for ages.

ALBERT: Poor Benny. He was always so tiresome.

They go out of earshot and finally disappear into the lift after pausing at the desk.

A PORTER *fetches their bags.* INEZ ZULIETA *and* VIOLET EMERY *enter from Lounge.*

INEZ: I'm going straight home.

VIOLET: Don't be so unreasonable.

INEZ: Unreasonable! (*She laughs bitterly.*) You seem to take a delight in making me utterly miserable.

VIOLET: You will imagine things.

INEZ: I don't imagine—I know.

VIOLET: You're impossible.

INEZ: Thank you.

They go out through the swing doors.

The HANCOX *family arrives,* MR. *and* MRS., *typical wealthy middle-class, and their daughter,* PHYLLIS.

HANCOX: Stay here while they bring in the luggage. I'll go and see about the rooms.

MRS. HANCOX: We'll sit down—Come, Phyllis.

She and PHYLLIS *come down stage and sit by the table. The* PORTER *is occupied with their luggage.* BERYL FLETCHER *appears from the direction of the lifts with* DOROTHY PRICE. DOROTHY *is less chic than she used to be.* BERYL *is radiant, wearing several expensive bangles and two or three strings of pearls.*

BERYL: My God, he isn't here. (*She looks around.*)

DOROTHY: Never mind, he will be in a minute.

BERYL: He knows I hate hanging about. Just wait, that's all. I'll teach him.

DOROTHY: Don't be silly, dear.

BERYL: Well, he's always doing things like this—annoying me.

DOROTHY: For heaven's sake don't have another scene with him—I can't bear it.

BERYL: He thinks he can do what he likes just because he's so damned rich.

DOROTHY: Here he is.

> EDGAR DARRELL *enters—thin and forty.*

BERYL (*disagreeably*): At last.

EDGAR: I'm sorry. I didn't know I was late.

BERYL: No, you never do know.

EDGAR: Hallo, Dorothy.

DOROTHY: Hallo.

EDGAR (*to* BERYL): Don't be unkind, little girl.

BERYL: Dorothy's coming to Deauville with us in July.

EDGAR (*despondently*): Oh, is she?

DOROTHY: Beryl said you wouldn't mind.

EDGAR: Of course I don't.

> *They go out through the swing doors.*
> MR. HANCOX *comes down from back.*

HANCOX: Come along.

PHYLLIS (*as they rise*): Mother.

MRS. HANCOX: What, dear?

PHYLLIS: Did you see her pearls?

MRS. HANCOX: Whose pearls?

PHYLLIS: That woman's—they were huge!

MRS. HANCOX: I suppose they'll send the trunks up later.

> *They all three go off upstage to the lifts.*
> CYRIL *enters through swing doors and comes over*
> *to* NORMA.

CYRIL: Pardon me, are you Mrs. Cyril Hardacre?

NORMA (*looking up*): Certainly not. How dare you address me!

CYRIL: Darling!

NORMA: You've been out far too long anyhow.

CYRIL: I've bought you a present.

NORMA: Cyril—that was awfully naughty of you.

CYRIL (*producing package from his pocket*): Here.

NORMA: No—wait until we go to our room.

CYRIL: I can't wait long—

NORMA: Baby.

CYRIL: Who are you writing to?

NORMA: Father.

CYRIL: Give him my love.

NORMA: Sit down—I shan't be a minute.

CYRIL: Very well. (*He sits down opposite to her and lights a cigarette.*)

NORMA: Light one for me.

CYRIL: All right. (*He does so.*) Here.

NORMA: Thanks, dear.

CYRIL: What have you said?

NORMA: Nothing much—just how happy I am.

CYRIL: Oh, is that all?

NORMA: There. (*She folds up the letter and addresses an envelope.*)

CYRIL: I've got the seats for to-night.

NORMA: Front row?

CYRIL: Yes.

NORMA: Lovely.

CYRIL: Are you really so happy?

NORMA (*seriously*): Yes.

CYRIL: Sure?

NORMA: Positive.

CYRIL: Oh, God!

NORMA: What's the matter?

CYRIL: It all seems too good to be true.

NORMA: I feel that, too—I didn't know I was going to love you quite so much.

CYRIL: Neither did I.

NORMA (*rising*): It's different from anything that's ever happened to me before. I'm going to be so careful to keep it always true and real like it is now.

CYRIL: We will both—darling.

NORMA: Come along up—I'm dying to see my present.

CYRIL: Pardon me, Mrs. Hardacre. (*He kisses her suddenly.*)

NORMA (*laughing*): Cyril! I'm sure that man saw us!

    They go off.

CURTAIN